LIFE
WITH
ROSE
KENNEDY

LIFE WITH ROSE KENNEDY

Barbara Gibson
with Caroline Latham

WARNER BOOKS

A Warner Communications Company

Copyright © 1986 by Barbara Gibson and Caroline Latham
Warner Books, Inc., 666 Fifth Avenue, New York, NY 10103

W A Warner Communications Company

Printed in the United States of America
First Printing: March 1986
10 9 8 7 6 5 4 3 2 1

Library of Congress Cataloging-in Publication Data

Gibson, Barbara.
   Life with Rose Kennedy.

   1. Kennedy, Rose Fitzgerald, 1890–   —Addresses,
essays, lectures   2. Kennedy family—Addresses, essays,
lectures.   3. Gibson, Barbara—Addresses, essays,
lectures.   4. Presidents—United States—Mothers—
Addresses, essays, lectures.   I. Latham, Caroline.
II. Title
E748.K378G53 1986   973.922′0924   85-43159
ISBN 0-446-51325-3

When Mrs. Kennedy once suggested to me that I keep a diary of my days working for her, she said, "It will be nice for your children to have, to look back on." And so, as Mrs. Kennedy suggested, I would like to dedicate this book to
>	*my children, Kathleen and Kevin,*
>	*and to their children,*
>	*and to posterity.*

Contents

LIFE WITH ROSE KENNEDY

1

Remembering Rose Kennedy

The last real conversation I had with Rose Kennedy was early in the summer of 1982. Although I had visited her only a few months before, I was shocked at the change in her. Her body seemed shriveled and terribly thin. The knuckles of her hands were so swollen that her wedding ring had been cut to help ease it off. Her memory was spotty, and I feared that perhaps she wouldn't remember me.

Her granddaughter Sydney Lawford took me out to the terrace of the Palm Beach house, where Mrs. Kennedy was sitting in the sun, swathed in several layers of clothes despite the balmy temperature. When Sydney told her grandmother I was there, it was obvious that she didn't recognize my name. But, seconds later, it was equally obvious that she did recognize my face. I gave her a kiss on the check and we began chatting.

I told Mrs. Kennedy about my current job as a private secretary to a wealthy Palm Beach businessman. I intended simply to be entertaining, but after she listened quietly for a few minutes, she remarked, "I can tell you don't like him by the expression on your face." I was surprised that she was still able to read my expressions so clearly. After all, it had been several years since we mutually agreed that she really needed

1

a nurse/maid/companion more than a secretary and I left her employ.

I answered that it wasn't so much that I didn't like him as it was that I didn't approve of the way he lavished gifts on his children and spent extravagantly on luxurious living. Mrs. Kennedy quickly responded, "Well, of course, that's personal. If he has a lot of money, he probably worked hard for it, so he should be able to spend it the way he chooses." I thought the comment humorous, in view of what I knew about her own spending habits and idea of thrift.

I had moved since the last time I stopped by to visit, so I told Mrs. Kennedy all about my new apartment and how much I was enjoying it. She didn't seem to recognize the address, but when I told her it was near the Seminole Golf Club, she perked up. "Oh, yes," she said enthusiastically, "the President used to play there. Mr. Kennedy played there also. We used to pack up the car with a picnic lunch and go there to spend the day." Her face lighted up as the memories came back to her.

At her age, it was not surprising that the past held more interest than the present or future. Yet she didn't indulge herself for long in looking back. She asked questions about a book I had read lately, and we discussed a report in the paper that in an upcoming TV movie about the Kennedys, the role of Rose Kennedy would be played by Katharine Hepburn. It amused me to think how frequently tall women were chosen to play the part of my former employer, who was just barely over five feet tall. It must be the power of her personality that made it seem appropriate to portray her as statuesque.

Sydney came back to remind Mrs. Kennedy that it was nearly time for the evening news on television. Although she was then in her early nineties, Mrs. Kennedy apparently kept up her interest in world events and maintained her customary clockwork schedule. She invited me to stay and watch the news with her; when I pleaded a previous engagement, she suggested I come back another day and swim with her. I was amazed and impressed to learn that she was still going in the pool every day. What an iron will she had!

I told her I would stop by again soon, and she squeezed my hand. As I walked back across the terrace, she suddenly called out to me, "Oh, Barbara, what was it you did for me?"

"I was your secretary, Mrs. Kennedy."

She answered thoughtfully, "Is that so . . ." and then there was a long pause.

"I seem," she said, "to remember a very pleasant association."

That's the way I remember it, too.

Working as secretary to Rose Kennedy was a job unlike any other. It made big demands, and it brought big rewards. There were times when I felt I would never understand my employer, and other times when I felt I understood her all too well. When I first began to work for her, I found her surprisingly easy to talk to, but difficult to feel close to. But as time passed, our relationship grew. Mrs. Kennedy was a feisty and independent woman who had never acknowledged that she needed anyone and wasn't going to start just because she was a frail octogenarian. Yet I recognized that she valued the closeness and companionship that developed between us, as did I. I never doubted that it was a privilege to share the candid thoughts of this spirited and critical old lady.

Today, whenever I meet people who know that I was once Rose Kennedy's personal secretary, they always ask the same question: "What's she really like?"

When I started working for Mrs. Kennedy, I knew no more than the mix of legend and history that everyone else knows. I knew that Mrs. Kennedy had once been Rose Fitzgerald, the beautiful daughter of Boston's turn-of-the-century mayor, John F. Fitzgerald, who was affectionately known to his constituents as "Honey Fitz" in honor of his persuasive way of speaking. Rose was still in her teens when she met Joseph Patrick Kennedy, only son of a Boston Irish publican who was also active in city politics, sometimes as Honey Fitz's ally and sometimes as his rival. Rose's father was opposed to the match, and the couple had to wait seven years before they could marry.

By the time of their marriage, Joe had already become a bank president. True, it was a small bank, and his father was one of the major stockholders, but it was still an early demonstration of Joe's business acumen and proved to be the first step in a long process of amassing wealth and power. Joe Kennedy was a stock speculator, a deal maker, a manipulator of stock prices (back in the days when such tactics were legal). He is rumored to have made money selling liquor during Prohibition, and it's certainly a fact that he made a considerable amount of money in the movie business.

While Joe was out conquering the world, Rose was at home raising the children. They had nine of them, so she was kept busy. The oldest child, Joseph P. Kennedy, Jr., was their pride and joy. According to most reports, Joe Jr. was a natural leader and like his father an aggressive man. The family expected great things of him, but their hopes were destroyed abruptly and painfully when Joe Jr. was killed on a dangerous bombing mission near the end of World War II.

The second child was John F. Kennedy. A somewhat frail and bookish child, he nevertheless did his best to live up to his parents' expectations and become a keen competitor in all arenas. When his older brother died, Jack became the focus of family hopes, and he began his political career as a congressman not long after World War II. The fact that he was a veteran, and a hero to boot—decorated for his efforts to save his crew when his PT boat sank in the South Pacific—didn't hurt his appeal to the voters. The rest is history, from the shining moments of Camelot to that dreadful day in Dallas and the sorrow the Kennedy family shared with the world. Although his widow, Jackie, remarried (to Greek shipping tycoon Aristotle Onassis), she and her two children, Caroline and John, remained a part of the Kennedy circle.

The third child was Rosemary, a beautiful girl who also brought her parents heartbreak. Early in her childhood, it became apparent that her development was unnaturally slow, and the Kennedys had to face the fact that Rosemary was retarded. They did their best to look for cures and help, and they also did their best to camouflage her condition. Eventually they had to admit defeat, and Rosemary was permanently placed in a convent, where she could be looked after by the nursing sisters.

The fourth child was Kathleen, a bright and vivacious girl who was always surrounded by friends and admirers. Kathleen had a great social success in London when her father was ambassador there, and finally she married the heir to the greatest English dukedom. Her husband was killed in action in World War II, only a few brief weeks after their marriage. Kathleen stayed with her family for the rest of the war, but as soon as peace was declared, she returned to live in England. She was killed a few years later in the crash of a small private plane during bad weather.

The fifth child was Eunice. She was a smart, tough, courageous girl; many observers thought that if she had been a boy, she would have been the most successful of all the Kennedy children. Eunice married Sargent Shriver, who at that time was employed by her father as the director of the Merchandise Mart, a huge retail complex in Chicago. Eunice and Sarge had five children: one daughter (Maria, now a cohost of *CBS Morning News*) and four sons. Sarge, who was the director of the Peace Corps during his brother-in-law's administration, was later appointed ambassador to France by Lyndon Johnson. He was George McGovern's running mate in 1972 and made an attempt to run on his own for the presidency in 1976. Since then, his political career has been in abeyance. Eunice remains extremely active in charitable affairs for the retarded, especially those sponsored by the Kennedy family foundation.

Sixth in line was Patricia. Pat married actor Peter Lawford, and the couple lived for some time in southern California. They had four children: one boy and three girls. The children were still relatively young when the marriage ended in divorce. Pat now lives in New York, where she is one of the stars of that city's social elite.

The seventh child was Robert F. Kennedy. As a small boy, he was doggedly determined to keep up with his older brothers, no matter how much effort it took. He made it into the Navy at the very end of World War II and then went to law school. Bobby was a devoted family man, very much in love with his wife, Ethel, and always trying to spend as much time as possible with his children. They had eleven of them, ranging from Kathleen Hartington Kennedy, who was the oldest of all the Kennedy grandchildren, down to daughter Rory, who was born months after Bobby's death. Bobby was his brother's attorney general and the one who inherited much of his political legacy when President Kennedy died. After a long struggle with an innate reluctance to step into his brother's shoes, Bobby finally decided to run for the presidency in 1968 . . . and tragically became the second Kennedy to fall victim to an assassin's bullets. Ethel and the younger children still occupy the same house in suburban Virginia and spend their summers at the Kennedy compound in Hyannis Port.

The eighth child of Joe and Rose Kennedy was Jean. She married Steve Smith, a shrewd businessman who became his father-in-law's right hand, helping him run the family business empire and taking over after his death. Jean and Steve have four children, two boys and two girls, and they live in New York, where they are socially prominent.

The ninth and last child was Edward M. Kennedy. The much-loved and often spoiled baby of the family, he grew into a charming and gregarious man, with a touch of the natural Irish political instincts of his grandfather. Ted also went to law school, and in 1962, while his brother was in the White House, he was elected U.S. senator from Massachusetts. Ted and his wife, Joan, had three children: Ted Jr., Kara, and Patrick. Ted seems to have weathered more tragedy than any one man could be expected to survive. Beyond the deaths of all three of his brothers, Ted has coped with a long period of hospitalization after a plane crash that left doctors convinced he would never walk again; the unfortunate events at Chappaquiddick that left Mary Jo Kopechne dead and his political career shadowed; the heartbreak of discovering that his son Teddy had bone cancer, which necessitated the amputation of his leg; and his wife's alcoholism, which required more support than perhaps he was able to give at the time. Ted and Joan were divorced in the early 1980s, but she still has the house only minutes away from the Kennedy compound in Hyannis Port, and Ted remains close to his children.

The raising of all her children was Mrs. Kennedy's chief concern. Her husband was away for long periods of time, occupied with business matters and, according to rumor, having affairs with a number of women, including a long and passionate one with Gloria Swanson. It was Rose who took the children to church, worried through their illnesses, meted out discipline for offenses such as unfinished homework or rude behavior. Years later, when her son became President, Mrs. Kennedy often told reporters about how she kept track of the major events in her children's lives by using an index card system on which she jotted down such things as dates of inoculations and their heights and weights on each birthday.

Through all this, the public came to have an image of Rose Kennedy that was, finally, too good to be true. At least she herself never took the public's conception of her too seriously, as I learned when I worked for her. I remember particularly one day when I picked her up after church (the chauffeur, as so often happened, was otherwise occupied). She was just inside the church doors, and as I walked in, she flicked me with a few drops of water from the small stoup nearby. "They tell me I'm a saint," she said wryly, "so this is my blessing." It is certainly true that many books and articles about the Kennedy family make Rose Kennedy out to be a minor saint, perpetually uncomplaining and self-sacrificing. But the Rose Kennedy I finally learned to know after years of living and working with her closely was considerably more interesting than that. Deeply religious and wholeheartedly dedicated to her family, she was nevertheless fully human, with the foibles and follies that condition implies for all of us.

One minute Rose Kennedy could step into the limelight, beautifully dressed and elegantly groomed, looking authentically glamorous and much younger than her eighty-odd years. Then this woman, who was revered by millions all over the world, would go off for her solitary walk, her solitary swim, her solitary trip to mass, spending most of her daily life all alone. She could be outspokenly critical, and yet she would never tell anyone when she felt sad or depressed. She worked her emotions out in the swimming pool, dog-paddling furiously from one end to the other as she tried to escape her sorrows. She could give away millions to the retarded and then try to return used bottles of nail polish for credit.

In other words, Rose Kennedy was a complex person. And I believe she wanted people to know it. She never fell for her own publicity, and in the end I think she wearied of it. She was a spunky old lady who could be full of vim and vinegar, and I think she was proud of the fact. I'm sure she would not like to be remembered as nothing more than saintly and silent. What about the headstrong woman who could glare at you for long minutes and then say fiercely, "Do as you're told"? What about the octogenarian who loved to dance and who sang Irish ballads at the top of her voice in kitchen duets with the cook? What about the woman who wore false eyelashes even when her hands were so shaky with age that it was hard to put them on? Those were a part of Rose Kennedy, too, and I think what I liked best about her was that she never tried to hide it.

Perhaps that was why she made such a point of encouraging me to keep a diary of my experiences in the years I was with her. "You'll never have another job like this one," she advised me, and she wanted to be sure I was keeping a record of it. At her urging, I did keep a diary, and I did save many boxes of papers and memorabilia. At the time, I was dubious about the usefulness of such records, but now I am glad I have them, because they help me jog my memory so I can paint an accurate picture of the real Rose Kennedy.

Mrs. Kennedy was quite aware of the fact that even when I worked for her, people frequently asked me what she was like. I remember one conversation we had about it: When I confirmed that it was true that people often asked me about her, she asked me eagerly what I said! I answered that she was too complex a personality to describe in a few short sentences. It would take a book. . . .

Here then is my answer to the question. See for yourselves the charming, aggravating, amusing, maddening, admirable woman who was Rose Kennedy.

2

What Does "the Secretary" Really Do?

As I pulled into the driveway of the Kennedy compound in Hyannis Port one summer day in 1974, I thought about my coming interview with Rose Kennedy, who was looking for a new private secretary. My own feelings about the job, then as now, could best be described as ambivalent.

How do you get to be the personal secretary of one of the world's most famous women? In my case, it was entirely accidental.

I had gone to live on the Cape in 1967 after my marriage ended. Our family had known happy times there during summer vacations, which is perhaps what made it attractive to me at that moment. I bought a comfortable house big enough for myself and my two children, Kathleen and Kevin, then school age. The cozy familiarity of life in a small town on the Cape seemed like just what we needed, after years of moving with my husband to such disparate places as Cleveland, Ohio, and Tokyo, Japan. We had all learned a lot from the traveling we had done, but I felt it was now time to put down some roots.

As soon as the three of us were settled, I began to look around for some kind of work to keep me busy and to supplement my income. When I was single, I had worked as a secretary in Washington, first for the FBI and then in the office of a congressman. My experience on Capitol Hill had prepared me for virtually anything . . . or so I thought until I met Mrs. Kennedy.

I found a part-time job doing secretarial work for a prominent local businessman; the convenient hours made it possible to see my children off to school in the morning and be there when they got home in the afternoon. There was a part-time bookkeeper in the office, who mentioned that she had formerly worked for "the Ambassador," as Joe Kennedy always liked to be called. Since his stroke in 1961, there had been no need for the large business staff he had once employed, but she still kept in touch with the remaining clerical staff at the compound. She knew that they were often overburdened by the work load of that busy family, especially in the spring of 1968, when Bobby was making his bid for the presidency.

Then came the tragic news of Bobby Kennedy's assassination at his victory celebration in the California primary. The increased volume of mail and renewed press attention on the entire family made it impossible for Mrs. Kennedy's secretary to keep up. Would I consider taking some work on?

The circumstances seemed ideal. I could pick up the typing work and do it at home in the late afternoons and evenings. It would bring in some extra money, and it might be fun, too; once again I would feel connected to world events. I told the bookkeeper I was interested.

Only a few days later I got a call from Mrs. Kennedy's secretary, Denise Smith, asking if I could come to her house that evening to pick up some work. When I got there, I thought the poor woman looked positively exhausted. Denise said she had been working six or seven days a week, and yet she was still far behind. Unwilling to keep up the demanding pace any longer, Denise was resigning. But she wanted at least to clear up the backlog of correspondence before a new secretary came on the scene. She gave me a pile of routine letters that needed only standard replies and dictated more personalized answers to other letter-writers. As I staggered to the door with my assignment, she cautioned me, "No one at the compound knows about this. I cleared it with the Kennedys' New York office, and you'll be paid directly by them. Don't tell Mrs. Kennedy!" It was by no means the only time I was to hear that warning.

Together we worked to clear up the backlog, and by the end of the summer, Denise was able to leave. The Kennedys, as usual, went to Palm Beach that fall, and I remained to winter over in gray Hyannis. But the following spring, I got a call from Mrs. Kennedy's new secretary, Diane Winter. Like Denise, she urgently needed help. I understood why as soon as I walked into the charming cottage the Kennedys had rented for her in Hyannis Port, just around the corner from the compound. Her entire living room was filled with stacks of file folders, unopened mail, packages, and newspapers. Diane moaned that some of the filing that needed to be done was more than two years old.

For the first few weeks of that summer, I went to Diane's house three nights a week to help her try to cope with the overflow. But someone must have decided that it was all right to tell Mrs. Kennedy about the work I was doing, because Diane soon suggested that I start coming to the Kennedys' house to do typing and filing there. A makeshift office was set up for me across the hall from Diane, in a little first-floor nook the family called the Golf Room because it was where they kept their clubs and golf shoes. I did my typing on an antiquated steno desk someone had dug up and my filing on the floor, where I could sort things into piles.

I was then only a secretary's secretary, but occasionally I caught sight of my real employer, Mrs. Kennedy. The first time she passed my door, she looked in and said, "Good afternoon. Diane tells me that you have two children. How lovely! How are they? Thank you for coming," and walked quickly on without waiting for a reply. She was dressed in a wide-brimmed straw hat, Bermuda shorts, white bobby socks, and funny black shoes that looked old-fashioned and "sensible." On most occasions when I subsequently caught sight of Mrs. Kennedy, she was on her way through the hall where I worked to the garage to get into her green Buick sedan and dash off to do an errand or play a round of golf.

At other times, I would catch sight of her walking across the wide front lawn that sloped down to the sea. Her small figure—Mrs. Kennedy was only about five-one—was almost obscured by the confusion of dogs, grandchildren, nurses, and domestics, yet she always seemed to be the focal point of the composition. She habitually acted calm and cheerful. Even in periods of great stress, her attitude was "business as usual." I remember that I had to go to the compound on the Sunday morning after the news of Chappaquiddick broke, to drop off eighty-five letters I had typed that needed Mrs. Kennedy's signature so they could go out Monday morning. Of course, I had heard the shocking news of Ted's accident on the radio that morning—or at least the sketchy details that were first released —and I was a bit apprehensive about what I would find when I got to the Kennedy house.

To my surprise, Mrs. Kennedy appeared quite serene. She and her daughter Pat were having breakfast together and talking normally about nothing in particular. Then I caught sight of Senator Kennedy walking out of Ethel Kennedy's house with a man whose face was unfamiliar to me, and the Senator was smiling in his usual jovial manner. It was my first glimpse of the famed Kennedy ability to remain outwardly unruffled no matter what the crisis. I would have thought it was just another summer Sunday at the compound if I hadn't later seen those same two men, now looking very worried, pacing the beach in coats and ties, quite obviously discussing the situation and how it should be handled.

My recollections of that summer of 1969 are nearly all pleasant ones. My office was packed with interesting memorabilia, including a charming painting by Jackie of all the children at Hyannis Port, standing on the jetty waving at the Ambassador's plane as it circled overhead. There were family snapshots and the framed historical treasures of a check signed by Thomas Jefferson and the first airmail letter flown into Surinam by a young pilot named Charles A. Lindbergh. The house was full of people coming and going, and out of the corner of my eye, I could watch the passing parade: Joan Kennedy looking very pretty and very pregnant; Bobby and Ethel's children Joe, Bobby, and David stopping by to see their grandparents; dogs passing in and out; the Senator striding through the front door of the house and calling out to his mother. Through my office window, which was adjacent to the kitchen, there wafted wonderful smells of baking cookies and big family feasts being prepared. Outside, there was the well-kept lawn, the blaze of flowers, and always the noise of children having fun.

Yet, in retrospect, I realize that the summer of 1969 was a hard one for Rose Kennedy. First there was the news of Jacqueline Kennedy's marriage to Aristotle Onassis, which brought a flood of correspondence, much of it hostile. Then there was Chappaquiddick, another event that created public dismay and private sorrow as well, both for the tragedy of the life lost and for the career shadowed. And underlying all the news of that summer was the obvious decline in the Ambassador's health. For years after his stroke, although he was unable to either walk or talk, Joe Kennedy remained very much the master of the house. Things were done his way; his comfort and convenience were the overriding imperatives; and his pleasure and approval were still anxiously sought. But by the summer of 1969, it was obvious that he was sinking, and that fact dominated the emotional atmosphere of the entire compound.

By the time the Ambassador died that fall, I was no longer working for the Kennedys. Discouraged by the heavy burden of Mrs. Kennedy's correspondence, I had found a full-time job elsewhere. My daily routine was now much calmer, but occasionally I missed the excitement of the days at the Kennedy compound. Still, I had never really known anyone there very well, neither family nor staff. The Kennedys were just another memory, a good topic of conversation at parties, a remembered highlight of my life, like the time some twenty years earlier when I had a chance to meet the Duke of Kent while on a skiing holiday in Austria.

I did make a point of keeping up with the news of the Kennedy family through Joe Gargan, who was a vice-president of the Hyannis bank where I later went to work. Joe was Rose Kennedy's nephew and Teddy Kennedy's companion since boyhood. Once or twice he had mentioned that the full-time job as Mrs. Kennedy's secretary was available (there seemed to be quite a turnover). But with my two children at home, the travel involved was impossible. And I still remembered the terrible burden of the work there.

Then, in the summer of 1974, Joe once again asked me if I would consider working as Mrs. Kennedy's secretary. At this point, the notion appeared more feasible. Since my children were now away at school, I would be able to travel back and forth between Palm Beach and Hyannis Port. But did I want to take on something as strenuous as the job of Rose Kennedy's secretary? I remembered those former secretaries who were virtually buried under the heavy load of the work involved. Surely the rapid turnover in that position was no mere coincidence. When I expressed these qualms to Joe Gargan, he reassured me. "Since Uncle Joe died and Aunt Rose had her stroke last February, things have definitely slowed down. It's a different job these days."

Just how different I was soon to learn for myself.

At Joe's urging, I called the latest secretary, Jay Sanderson, to set up an appointment to see Mrs. Kennedy. Jay had recently become engaged and was anxious to locate a suitable replacement so she could leave to be married. She said she was sure I would find the job much easier these days than I remembered it and suggested that she schedule an interview for me with Mrs. Kennedy right away. "Let's make it for some time after work," she said. "Mrs. Kennedy will be impressed with the fact that you are too hardworking and prudent to take time off from your present employer."

I dressed for that 8:00 P.M. interview with great care, hoping my navy blazer and white skirt would strike the right balance between professionalism and the modesty appropriate to secretaries. Instinct told me to enter the house through the rear service entrance, as I had always done when I worked there before. I was greeted by a maid, who introduced herself as Jeannette and added, to forestall confusion, that Mrs. Kennedy always pronounced her name "Janet." She showed me into the living room, and then I heard Mrs. Kennedy's familiar voice call down from the head of the stairs, "Is the guest here?"

She came down immediately. I stood and smiled as she made her entrance, dressed in a short-sleeved white suit I recognized from a picture of her on the cover of *Look* a few years earlier, along with suitable costume jewelry and what seemed like a lot of makeup for an elderly lady. I stepped forward and offered my hand. She grasped it warmly, saying, "Sit here with me on the couch, dear." I learned later that the couch was held in high esteem, since it was the one in the Kennedy house in Bronxville, New York, on which Cardinal Pacelli had sat when he came to tea a few years before he became Pope Pius XII. To Mrs. Kennedy, it was ever after a treasured memento.

I had been somewhat nervous about this interview with the famous Rose Kennedy, who had always before seemed so distant, and it didn't help that she turned up looking exactly like a picture on a magazine cover. Yet, to my great surprise, I found her very easy to talk to. She quickly made me feel comfortable, and the questions she asked me about myself seemed interested rather than threatening. She mentioned, as she looked at my résumé, that she didn't remember I had worked there in the past. I said it was in the summer of 1969 (the labors of 1968 were still a secret). She replied, "Of course, that was the year Mr. Kennedy died," and then her voice trailed off and she looked into space for a few minutes as the burden of memories came back to her.

Suddenly snapping back to the present, Mrs. Kennedy mentioned that her need was for a social secretary. Would my business experience be appropriate for dealing with the kind of correspondence I would have to handle? I suggested that to give her reassurance, I would type up a sample letter. To do so, we walked through the back hall to the secretary's room, where I went to the desk and took out a piece of Mrs. Kennedy's gray

17

stationery, engraved by Cartier's. This familiarity surprised her, especially in view of her own repeated protest that she knew nothing about the "office."

Mrs. Kennedy gave me a hypothetical case of someone who had invited her to attend a luncheon and asked me to write a letter declining the invitation. She was happy with my finished letter, but I wasn't, for I noticed how faint the ink was. "There's something wrong with the ribbon on this typewriter, Mrs. Kennedy," I said. "It's so pale, I think it needs to be changed." She took the letter again, adjusted her glasses to look at it more carefully, and agreed, "Yes, you're right, it does." She seemed delighted that I had discovered a flaw, and from that moment, it was clear that she wanted me to be her secretary.

"The hours are nine to five. Mr. Kennedy always liked the secretaries to be in the house all day, so Janet will fix lunch for you here." She paused, and her next words seemed just a bit disgruntled. "I don't know what the pay is. You'll have to settle all that with the New York office." With that, the business discussion was over. "Do you think you'll enjoy going to Florida in the winters?" she asked almost teasingly.

"It should be nice to escape the winters on the Cape," I responded, "and I have relatives there I'll enjoy seeing."

In a flash, the atmosphere changed. "Yes, well, of course, that's personal," she said distantly. For Mrs. Kennedy, there was a wall of privacy around any personal matter—mine, hers, or anyone else's—and she didn't intend to see it breached. After a moment, she showed me politely to the door (the rear door, so I knew I had guessed right about the status of "the secretary") and said she would like me to start as soon as possible.

Later, when I replayed the conversation in my mind, I worried about whether I was doing the right thing in accepting the job. Would the work be too much for me? Would Mrs. Kennedy? Still, I had by this time worked in enough offices to know how dreary a more conventional job could be. I hoped working for Mrs. Kennedy would give me an occasional taste of fun and the chance to meet some interesting people. Moreover, the compensation, when finally discussed with the New York office, sounded good. Not only would I get a reasonable salary, but the New York office would provide a place to live in both Palm Beach and Hyannis Port; I could sell or rent my own house and live rent free. They would also pay me for the mileage put on my car doing errands for Mrs. Kennedy and driving back and forth from Massachusetts to Florida. So I decided to take the job—and do my best to get all the fun out of it that I could.

I have to admit that my brave resolution was a bit shaken when I got together with the departing secretary for dinner before she left. Jay gave me a long set of instructions about how to handle the job. And my employer.

"Your day starts at nine o'clock when you arrive at the post office. And be sure you leave on the dot of five," Jay said sternly. "Otherwise, you'll find that your hours simply get longer and longer. Establish the precedent that you go out to lunch every day. There's never anything to eat in the refrigerator, and the maid will *not* cook for you. And whatever you do, don't agree to live in the house or in the apartment over the garage, even for a short period, or your life will never be your own."

Jay explained that the last few secretaries had made some changes to lighten the work load. Many letters could be answered with a simple engraved card one of them had devised, which said: "Mrs. Kennedy appreciates your interest and regrets that she is unable to answer her mail personally." She mentioned that after Mrs. Kennedy's stroke in 1973, the doctor had decided it was necessary to protect her from any worry. So I was to show her only three or four pieces of mail a day—just the ordinary personal correspondence she would enjoy—and handle the rest myself without telling her. She was to see only bills under thirty-five dollars. Everything else I was to approve and send directly to New York, where it would be paid out of Mrs. Kennedy's account.

I got the feeling there was more Jay could have told me. But she was anxious to leave and be married, and I was supposed to start immediately. So she wished me good luck and assured me that I would learn all about the job as I went along.

19

She was right. But what I learned was not exactly what I had expected.

My first few days on the job were extremely puzzling. For one thing, I couldn't understand what had happened to the staff I had seen in the house back in 1968 and 1969. In those days, the bustling household was supported by a cook, two maids, a gardener, a chauffeur, a secretary, and of course a round-the-clock nursing staff for the Ambassador. Now the elderly Jeannette turned out to be the sole person working inside the house. She alone did the cooking and all the cleaning for the fifteen-room house and its occupants, and she also looked after Mrs. Kennedy and her clothes. The extent of her chores clearly explained why she told me firmly she would not cook for me no matter what Mrs. Kennedy's instructions were about eating my lunch at the house. How could she spare the time? With all the work she had to do, it wasn't surprising that she put her foot down about taking on more. Outside, there was only Arthur, who served as gardener, chauffeur, handyman, and keeper of the keys for all three of the houses in the compound: Mrs. Kennedy's, Ethel's, and Jackie's. He, too, had his hands full, especially since Mrs. Kennedy had given up driving herself, after a minor accident that frightened everyone in the family. Occasionally men were hired by the day to do heavy cleaning and odd jobs, but day in and day out, the work of taking care of that big place fell on just two people. According to the local gossip, Mrs. Kennedy had fired the entire staff after her husband's funeral, saying she could no longer afford to keep so many people on the payroll.

Another thing that puzzled me was why Mrs. Kennedy was alone so much of the time. It was July, the height of the summer season, and the whole family was gathering in their respective homes. Ethel was next door with all of her younger children, and Jackie was at her house with its backyard bordering on Ethel's. The Shrivers were only a few minutes' drive away, and Teddy and his family were at Squaw Island, out at the tip of Hyannis Port yet still within walking distance for the active Kennedy family. Yet with all those people around, Mrs. Kennedy still spent most of her day by herself and ate her meals alone.

Most puzzling of all was the total lack of security at the compound, and most particularly at Mrs. Kennedy's house. During the peak of the tourist season, the town posted a guard on weekdays only, at the head of the dead-end street that leads into the compound, motivated at least as much by a desire to prevent traffic jams of goggling tourists as to protect the Kennedys. In the daytime, Arthur might be around to deal with intruders, unless he was driving Mrs. Kennedy somewhere, or way down at the other end of the property doing yard work. At night, there was no one in the big old house except for Mrs. Kennedy and Jeannette, who slept in—two elderly women all alone. The house was rarely locked; and even when it was, there were so many doors and windows in this oversize cottage by the sea that breaking in would have been child's play (as some of the grandchildren were later to demonstrate).

All in all, Mrs. Kennedy seemed curiously unprotected for a woman whose family had been the subject of public interest and private fantasy for so many years. One day, when Jeannette was off, Mrs. Kennedy and I were chatting in the kitchen as she made her own lunch of reheated creamed chicken (after refusing my offer of help). The two of us were alone in the house. Arthur was nowhere to be seen, and no one else appeared to be around the compound. "Mrs. Kennedy," I asked impulsively, "doesn't it worry you to be alone like this? Anyone could just walk in on you here in the kitchen."

"Nonsense," she replied with spunk. "No one would try anything with me." Then she added more thoughtfully, "I am an old woman, and the consequences would not be that great." She closed the conversation by strolling over to the refrigerator and taking out a dish of cold custard, which she promptly devoured with good appetite. Taking a few of her favorite sugar cookies from the tin on the counter, she went upstairs for her afternoon nap. Clearly she had no fears for her own safety . . . but I wondered if maybe the rest of the family sometimes worried about her there alone.

A few weeks later, my concern about this issue intensified, when it was discovered that a young woman was following Mrs. Kennedy back and forth to church and also trailing her on her long late-afternoon walks. One morning I found the woman sitting on the porch of the house that had been rented for me a few blocks away from Mrs. Kennedy's. When I got into my car, I found some papers she had left there—incoherent notes full of underlinings and exclamation marks. It turned out that she was an emotionally disturbed person who had decided she had to talk to Senator Kennedy about saving the world, and she thought his mother could lead her to him. The next time Teddy came to the compound, the woman caught sight of him. Having been briefed on the situation, he talked with her quietly for a few minutes in his car. Not long after that, she was taken away for psychiatric observation. I always thought it was both brave and kind of the Senator to talk to her, which made the eventual denouement all the more surprising: The young woman's father attempted to sue the Kennedy family for causing his daughter's emotional problems.

Gradually I began to realize how little of my time with Mrs. Kennedy would really be devoted to secretarial tasks. Although my day always began at the post office as I picked up the mail (the quantity sometimes required several trips back and forth to the car), it turned out that the mail was only the first and not the most important task of the day. I tried to sort it out roughly when I first came in, at the same time that Mrs. Kennedy returned from morning mass and had her breakfast in the dining room. By the time she was back upstairs in her bedroom, I had found the few personal letters I thought she might be interested in, and I was ready to go up to her room when she buzzed for me on the telephone intercom. That was the last moment of my day that could even be called routine.

From then on, the schedule was up to Mrs. Kennedy—and the results could definitely be unexpected. She might tell me to look up a word in the dictionary and type up the definition on a sheet of paper for her to memorize so she would be sure to use the word correctly. Or she might want to review some

sketches she had requested from Paris designers for outfits she would buy on her trip there in the fall. She might issue instructions to call Eunice, Pat, and Jean and ask them to come look at some Sandwich glass they might like to have. She often asked me to drive her into town, where she would shop for underwear, or get her hair done, and perhaps attend midday mass if for some reason she had missed her regular morning attendance. There was a thank-you note to write to the nuns of the Sacred Heart convent who had sent her a cake (angel food, of course); an appointment to arrange for someone who wanted to take a picture of the needlepoint piano bench cover made by Mrs. Kennedy's mother so it could appear in a book written by a friend of Jackie's; Pat Lawford's glasses, which she had left on her last visit, to be packed up and sent to her; a frantic search for the keys to Jackie's house when her burglar alarm suddenly went off at an incredible volume that could be heard all over Hyannis Port. Such crises were all in a day's work.

I also learned that I was sometimes going to have to act as Mrs. Kennedy's bodyguard. One afternoon I was working peacefully in my office when I heard loud noises coming from the dining room. I walked into the hall, and to my consternation saw a tall black man—I'm sure he couldn't have been shorter than six-five—strolling toward me. I drew myself up to my full five feet two inches and demanded to know who he was and how he had gotten into the house. He said he was collecting for charity and that when no one answered his knock at the rear door, he had simply walked in. Using the calmest voice I could manage under the circumstances, I told him this was a private residence and that he should speak to the gardener about any solicitation. Unfortunately the intruder showed no signs of departing. To my great relief, Arthur himself appeared at that moment, with the guard from the corner in tow. Their joint presence convinced the man to leave, and I breathed a sigh of relief.

Suddenly Mrs. Kennedy appeared at the head of the stairs, nostrils dilated and eyes blazing—a look I was to become quite familiar with. "I thought I told you to call me in time for my appointment," she said angrily. I looked at my watch and realized that she was right, I was several minutes late. Not wanting to alarm her unduly, I simply said that someone had come to the door and I had to make sure he was taken care of. She snapped, "I'm supposed to know about everything here. This is my house and that's what I'm here for." As I apologized, I thought to myself she seemed to intuit that something untoward had happened. As I was to learn in forthcoming years, it was not easy to deceive Rose Kennedy, no matter how kindly one's motives.

As time went by, I began to think of my position as being not so much that of secretary as of a lady-in-waiting. For example, since there was no maid to help Mrs. Kennedy with her clothes, I was the one to assist her in dressing when she made a public appearance: do up the tiny buttons, give an opinion about the choice of hat, perhaps help smooth out the rouge if she had applied it with too heavy a hand. Often I walked her to the car and waved her out of sight; just as often I myself might drive her where she was going. I tried to make a point of greeting her when she returned from some public event and helping her hang up the expensive Paris originals she wore for such occasions before she settled in for a restorative nap. Sometimes it seemed like a court ritual we were playing out.

Even when I accompanied Mrs. Kennedy, my lady-in-waiting status decreed that I tactfully remain a few steps behind. Jeannette had made this aspect of my duty clear from the outset. "If Mrs. Kennedy asks you to go into church with her some morning, be sure to sit in one of the pews at the back. She doesn't like to have people sitting up in front with her." In fact, she rarely asked me to attend with her, but she did sometimes ask that I come along and wait outside until she emerged. The church had both a front and a side door, and Mrs. Kennedy used them interchangeably, so I often incurred her wrath by being at the wrong door. I was the one who was supposed to be standing there waiting, not her!

Nowhere was that lady-in-waiting feeling stronger than in Mrs. Kennedy's own house. Apparently it had long been a custom for her children and grandchildren to stand as she entered a room. So when she and I would set off to do an errand or check up on something around the house, visitors would bob up and down as we passed—me always walking a respectful distance behind Mrs. Kennedy. This happened even when she went out to the pool. All the relatives lounging around would suddenly leap to their feet to acknowledge her presence as I followed carrying her towel and robe. I am not exaggerating when I say that even the people *in* the pool tried to stand up.

A lady-in-waiting was supposed to supply companionship when it was needed and, just as important, to recognize when it wasn't. It was only my second day on the job when Mrs. Kennedy asked me if I would like to swim with her. I said I would love to, but I didn't have a bathing suit with me. When she assured me that she could find an old suit that would fit me, I realized that she was genuinely eager to have company.

Together we walked down that famous path to the sea, where the Kennedys had so often been photographed. As we waded into the water, I began to have second thoughts. It was after all only early July, and the North Atlantic waters of Nantucket Sound were still rather chilly. When I shivered and squealed, Mrs. Kennedy said firmly, "Posh, this isn't cold. I grew up swimming in the Maine waters, and this feels warm by comparison." I wondered about the advisability of her swimming in such cold water, for I knew she had had a stroke the year before and I had seen in the files instructions from her doctor that she was not to swim in water colder than eighty-six degrees. Yet there she was, bobbing happily around in the calm ocean. So I plunged in to paddle by her side. She was very gay and lighthearted that afternoon, and I thought to myself, "It would have been fun to know her when she was younger." I had the feeling the young Rose Kennedy would have made a good friend, the kind who could turn even ordinary everyday life into a bit of a lark. That afternoon was the first time I heard her endearing, really quite girlish giggle—a sound I would grow to cherish.

We often swam together after that, especially in Palm Beach, where there was rarely a member of the family to go in with her. I enjoyed it because she was a good companion during those times. Besides, what office job can offer you the perk of a daily swim, either in the ocean or an Olympic-size heated pool? And in addition to the health and beauty benefits, I got to chat familiarly with Rose Kennedy—not a bad way to spend an hour of a working day!

Shortly after we began to swim together, Mrs. Kennedy one day suggested that I have lunch with her. It was lovely sitting at the old polished table, carefully placed in front of the dining room windows to get the best view of the sea, and chatting with Mrs. Kennedy throughout our leisurely hot meal of broiled chicken and rice and pureed carrots. But that day proved to be my only opportunity for such enjoyment. Jeannette, who had silently set a place for me when instructed to do so by Mrs. Kennedy, caught me almost immediately after lunch to protest. She didn't intend to wait on other staff members, she reiterated, and if the matter came up again, she would complain to Mrs. Kennedy. I didn't want to turn the situation into a crisis, so the next time Mrs. Kennedy asked me to join her for lunch, I said that I thought Jeannette didn't like it and I would go out for lunch as usual. She made some sharp remark about how she would run her own house any way she wanted to. But in fact she dropped the matter, and no further lunch invitations were proffered. I had the feeling she would have liked the company but she knew she would pay dearly for disturbing the domestic equilibrium.

That incident illustrated one of the difficult aspects of the job. As Mrs. Kennedy's private secretary, I necessarily became acquainted with many intimate details of her life. I saw her private face rather than her public one, and that inevitably made me feel emotionally involved. It was not easy to think of working for Mrs. Kennedy as just another job, or one of the world's most respected women as just another boss. By the end of my first week, I had already grown very protective of Mrs. Kennedy and very concerned about her welfare. I became upset when I thought people were not considering her wishes or looking after her health properly. It was necessary to work at reminding myself that Mrs. Kennedy was not a favorite elderly aunt but rather my current employer.

I believe Mrs. Kennedy, too, found it difficult to maintain the emotional distance of an employer. Yet she knew the dangers of becoming attached to people whose presence was only temporary, for the one or two or three years they might remain in her employ. In many ways, Mrs. Kennedy was a very warm and very caring human being, and that inner warmth often prompted her to disregard the fact that I was "the secretary" and reach out to me with friendly gestures. Then she would remember that I just worked there and that, like the long string of secretaries before me, I would probably be leaving in a matter of months. So she would bend over backward to establish the difference between personal and professional.

An example came that first summer in Hyannis Port when Carol Channing, who was appearing at the Cape's Melody Tent, paid a visit to Mrs. Kennedy. Carol was a friend of Mrs. Kennedy's daughter Eunice. She was always very nice about offering tickets to everyone in the compound, including the staff, who wanted to see her show. Thanks to her kindness, I had tickets to see it later in the week, so I was looking forward to getting an up-close glimpse of the star herself.

Mrs. Kennedy, Eunice, and Carol sat chatting in the big wicker chairs on the veranda, enjoying the sunshine and the wonderful view of the sea. After a while, Ethel came over with two of her children, Joe and little Rory, to join the group. While they were all gathered outside, I happened to walk by the maid's dining room, where I spotted Jeannette sitting tranquilly. I asked her if she was going to serve them something to drink, like lemonade or ice tea. "No," she answered flatly. "I'm not a serving maid. I don't have the right uniform. Besides, I'm too busy doing everything else around the place." I had read in a magazine somewhere that Carol Channing was a health-food addict who always brought her own food and drink along with her when she went to parties. For her sake, I hoped she had brought something with her on this visit, because it was obviously the only way she was going to get any nourishment.

After a while, Mrs. Kennedy brought Carol in to look at the family photos and mementos that covered every available inch of wall space in the sun-room. Since my office not only adjoined the sun-room but actually had a door opening into it, I was excited by the prospect of getting a chance to see the star in person. I heard footsteps approaching my door—and then, to my chagrin, I saw Mrs. Kennedy's hand reach across and close it firmly. The incident made me realize that whatever kind of personal rapport Rose Kennedy and I might succeed in establishing, there would always remain in Mrs. Kennedy's eyes a gap in our roles. To her, we were employer and employee, madam and staff.

It was interesting to see how the rest of the family regarded my status. Both Ethel and Jackie were extremely courteous, not just at our first meeting but always. Ethel, trimly dressed in navy slacks with a matching cardigan tied around her shoulders, introduced herself and shook my hand. Jackie, whom I first met as she came strolling back from the beach in a small but very becoming bikini, said, "Oh, you must be Gramma's new secretary, Barbara," and went on to make a few minutes of polite conversation.

This was in marked contrast to the reception I got from the Shrivers. The first time I met Eunice, I was sitting in Mrs. Kennedy's bedroom discussing a letter. Eunice ran in and without apology interrupted our conversation to ask her mother about plans for her upcoming birthday celebration. She was wearing shorts and an old white T-shirt, and she had apparently just washed her hair without bothering to take the time to comb out the tangles or smooth it away from her eyes. When their conversation was finished, she simply turned on her heel and left the room as abruptly as she'd entered it. I was surprised she didn't nod or glance in my direction; she came and went as if I weren't there at all. Her husband, Sarge, had an even odder response to meeting me, when I ran into him one day in the hallway. I knew who he was, of course, from photographs, but I assumed he didn't know who I was and that the proper thing to do would be to introduce myself. "Hello," I said, smiling, "I'm Barbara Gibson, Mrs. Kennedy's new secretary." He glanced at me briefly. "Well, lah-dee-*dah*," he said, and kept on walking.

28

By my second week on the job, I had met nearly all the members of the family, as they gathered in Hyannis Port to celebrate Mrs. Kennedy's birthday on July 22. There was to be a big clambake on the front lawn, and the plans and preparations were swirling all around me. The volume of mail suddenly picked up, as friends and strangers sent their best wishes. I counted more that 450 cards alone, not to mention the constant deliveries of presents and flowers. I showed a stack of cards to Mrs. Kennedy, who said with a glint of triumph, "I should be the one who's running for office!" The morning of the day itself, when the tour boats passed in front of the compound, they each dropped anchor and all the tourists aboard sang "Happy Birthday." She enjoyed stepping out on the porch to acknowledge the tribute with a wave.

I commented on all the excitement her birthday seemed to be creating, and she said sagely, "All this will soon calm down. . . . and then something else will happen. This is a big family, and there is always some kind of excitement."

Most of the time I spent with Mrs. Kennedy was very rewarding. I loved to listen to her comments on current events. That summer was the time of the Watergate scandal, which she followed closely and with great interest. Rather than rejoicing in the Republican scandal, she thought about the personal tragedies. "All those men," she said to me one day, "what will their families do?" Later she remarked approvingly, "Mrs. Ford has a very nice smile. They make a nice-looking couple." Prince Charles was much in the news that summer, and about him she said simply, "Everyone has their own destiny. They just have to work it out."

In fact, she was a keen observer of everything that passed before her. From her windows at "the big house" in the compound, she was able to see everything that was going on, and she was quick to comment. Once, after seeing Sandy Eiler, the stout man whom the Shrivers had for several years hired as a sort of athletic director for all the kids in the summer, she dictated this note to Sarge: "Please tell Sandy to start wearing a shirt. I am sick and tired of looking at his navel. Every year it becomes more prominent." She watched Ethel's children pedaling around the circular drive in front of her house in a small open racing car. "Call Ethel's house," she asked me, "and tell them to please put that contraption away in the garage. I told them last summer I did not want to see the children playing in it because it is too dangerous, and I'm not going to tell them again." I made the call to Ethel's secretary and relayed the message, and almost immediately there was no small vehicle to be seen.

Although Mrs. Kennedy was sometimes a bit imperious, she could also be very warm and friendly. I was touched by her evident enjoyment of our conversations about the latest fashions or some new kind of makeup that was being advertised for its revolutionary benefits. Sometimes I had to pinch myself to remember that this was a woman in her eighties, because she was still so interested in every detail of her appearance. At times, Mrs. Kennedy could also be rather maternal. On one of the rare days when she didn't feel up to swimming, she encouraged me to go in alone, which I did, enjoying the soothing motion of the summer-warm ocean. When I emerged from the water and headed up the path toward the house, I saw Mrs. Kennedy waving to me from the porch. "Yoo-hoo," she called, "are you all right?" She had put off taking her nap so she could watch over me all that time. I felt both happy and embarrassed (especially since this whole episode was being avidly watched by a boatload of tourists passing in front of the compound).

One day when Mrs. Kennedy and I were enjoying the bright sunshine as we paddled around in the bay, I told her how much I appreciated the chance to swim with her regularly and what a pleasure it was to have so varied a routine on the job. But I added that I was worried that I would slip behind in the typing and filing and correspondence. She looked at me with a wonderful sparkle in her eye and said, "Don't worry about the mail or the filing. Just keep me happy."

I tried my best.

3

Mrs. Kennedy and "the Children"

To my surprise, Mrs. Kennedy's children seemed to be almost as much in awe of her as I was. The more I watched their behavior in her presence, the more convinced I became that they, too, respected her greatly. They were just as susceptible as the rest of us to that look of disdain she could assume.

Sometimes I found it hard to believe that her children were so daunted. After all, although she called them "the children," they were in their forties and fifties. Eunice Shriver, Pat Lawford, Jean Smith, and Ted Kennedy were fully mature individuals with significant accomplishments and responsibilities of their own. They themselves had almost grown children; they were independently wealthy; they held important positions in government and administered a major charity. A scan of the media proved that they were frequently photographed, looking appropriately cool and self-assured, mingling unselfconsciously with the rich, famous, and powerful.

But back in their mother's house, these world-renowned figures reverted to the status of children, seeking to please the woman who to them symbolized the powerful authority of the adult world. That frail octogenarian, who weighed less than one hundred pounds and stood barely over five feet tall, easily dominated them all.

I first noticed this situation only a few weeks after I began working for Mrs. Kennedy. She and I were up in the attic of the Hyannis Port house, a storehouse of family treasures and trifles where Mrs. Kennedy sometimes spent hours sifting through the past. She had asked Eunice to join us to take a look at something she was considering giving away. (Jackie once astutely observed that "Gramma is never going to be happy until she gets that attic totally cleared out.") Eunice was fidgeting impatiently as her mother and I sorted through a pile of neatly labeled boxes, and her obvious restlessness attracted Mrs. Kennedy's attention. "Be still, Eunice," she snapped, using just the voice in which you might address a rambunctious child. Eunice —then fifty-three years old, the mother of five children, the wife of a former ambassador, the capable and energetic head of the Special Olympics and other successful programs for the retarded—obediently backed into a corner and didn't move again.

Over the next few years, I was to see continual evidence of the combination of respect and awe all Mrs. Kennedy's children had for her. "Don't tell Mother" was for all intents and purposes the motto of the family. For example, once in Palm Beach, Pat Lawford borrowed her mother's almost new Lincoln Continental for a quick trip to the Publix supermarket. In the parking lot, someone backed into her and scraped the side of the car. "Don't tell Mother," she insisted when she got home. "I don't want to upset her. Let's just get the car fixed without telling her." That was easier said than done. Mrs. Kennedy went to mass every morning and often went shopping on Worth Avenue in the afternoons as well. There was no way the absence of the car would go unnoticed. Finally the chauffeur and I worked out an elaborate system by which the car was always parked so that Mrs. Kennedy would get in on the side without the dent. This charade went on for several weeks, until Mrs. Kennedy went to Washington for a few days and the car could finally go into the shop. In the end, she never did find out about that dent.

"Don't tell Mother," said Jean Smith as she asked me to try to get a telephone line installed in the guest bedroom she always used when she visited Hyannis Port. "Don't tell Mother," I was cautioned one hot day when Eunice fainted on the pier and fell into Nantucket Sound. "Don't tell Mother," said Pat on giving me two bottles of wine from the supply of Beaujolais Villages that was her private stock in Palm Beach. The number of things I was not to tell "Mother" multiplied as the months went by.

Unquestionably Mrs. Kennedy loved her children. She once said to me, right out of the blue, "You know, it's funny. You would cut your arm off for your child," and then laid her own arm on the kitchen table. After a thoughtful pause, she added sadly, "But you would do nothing for your mother." To her, this difference was a simple fact. All her life, she had made her children's welfare her first priority, and even in her eighties, she continued to try to watch over them. When she thought it advisable, she didn't hesitate to intervene in their affairs. At an age when many women are content to hand over their responsibilities to the next generation and sit back in their rocking chairs, Mrs. Kennedy remained not just independent, but still fiercely maternal—still, as her son Jack had once expressed it, "the glue that held the family together."

Yet along with her love came what she believed to be a mother's inalienable right to criticize. Perhaps that was what made her children so anxious about her opinions. In their individual ways, they tried their best to please her.

Teddy Kennedy, her youngest child and only surviving son, seemed to be the most successful in achieving that goal. It was obvious that the bond between mother and son was a very special one. With him, she was always at her sparkling best. When Pat or Jean or Eunice came to visit her, she appeared for the family lunch ready for her nap, in her usual pink pajamas and a dressing gown. But when the Senator (as she always like to hear him called) was expected, she would dress in one of her vivid suits from Courrèges and even put on a matching wide-brimmed hat to preside over the table. Her manner with her son was almost flirtatious: She assumed a coquettish walk and something of a little-girl voice. She seemed to bask in his warmth, and she often commented that Teddy was the only one of her children to inherit her own father's wonderful sense of humor.

It was true that the Senator could be extremely charming. When I first met him, I was impressed by how much more handsome he looked in person than in photographs. To be perfectly truthful, I thought he was one of the sexiest men I had ever met! I was sure the reports of his career as a ladies' man were not exaggerated; he both looked and behaved the part. And he could be very funny . . . not so much by telling jokes as by seeing the humorous side of everyday life. One morning in Palm Beach, as the whole group was setting out for mass, the cook was the last to appear, and she had to squeeze into the front seat between Teddy and the chauffeur. "I can tell you're not a ninth child," he teased. "You don't know how to push your way in." He could even be funny in writing. In the files, I ran across a hilarious letter he had written to all the ushers at his brother Jack's wedding. His cook showed me a postcard he had sent her from England, showing the troops at the changing of the guard at Buckingham Palace and on the back the droll message, "I have invited all these men to lunch when I return."

Yet even Teddy came in for his fair share of critical comments from his mother. Many of them were about his weight, since Mrs. Kennedy (herself a lifelong dieter) considered excess poundage practically a mortal sin. When the Senator came to Palm Beach, Nellie the cook always made his favorite dessert, a chocolate roll of rich fudgy cake that was carefully rolled up with thick whipped cream. When he showed signs of wanting a second helping, his mother would scold him like a little boy. His response was equally boyish. He would accept the reprimand with a blush and then after dinner slip out to the kitchen to help himself to another slice of the calorie-laden dessert. "Don't tell Mother," he would warn Nellie as he gobbled down his forbidden treat.

Mrs. Kennedy also corrected her son's grammar when she detected an error. In a speech on the danger of drugs that he made while testing the waters for the 1976 presidential campaign, the Senator began a sentence with "If I was President . . ." His mother promptly fired off a letter dissecting his mistake: Since he was discussing something that was contrary to fact, he should say "If I *were* President . . ." She had me type this up neatly on her best white stationery with the blue border, and then she used one of her favorite ploys for backing a step away from the responsibility of writing the letter. She told me to add in the bottom left corner that the letter had been "dictated but not read," and I signed her name as her secretary. Teddy was so amused by this missive that he had it framed and mounted on the wall of his Senate office.

But not all of her criticisms of her son could be taken so lightly. One day, for some reason, the topic of Chappaquiddick happened to come up. Mrs. Kennedy said quite frankly, "The whole thing was so stupid. I don't blame people for thinking what they did. Mr. Kennedy always told the boys, 'Never go to parties alone. If you want to be in politics, you can't sit in the Stork Club every night with a girl on your arm. Make up your mind.' " In 1980, she once again criticized her son's public behavior. "I don't like to see him run against Carter," she told me when I stopped to visit her in Hyannis Port (I was no longer working for her at that time). "It breaks up the party."

It was clear that a major reason for Mrs. Kennedy's underlying favoritism toward Teddy was that he was a man, in a family that was conditioned (by Joe Kennedy, I gathered) to accept male dominance. I remember a speech she made in the ballroom of Boston's Sheraton Hotel when Teddy was campaigning for re-election to the Senate in 1978. She first amused her audience by telling them how critical many people were when they learned she was to have a ninth child, after it seemed the family was complete. "They warned me I would lose my figure, I would be tied down for years to come, I would never escape the demands of such a large family." Then, after a dramatic pause, she shifted the mood entirely by concluding somberly that if she hadn't had a ninth child, she would not today have a son. I looked around and there was not a dry eye in the audience. Later that year she underscored her views on the dominance of the male sex in a letter to her granddaughter Kathleen, saying that she would rather be known as the mother of a great man than to be a great woman herself. I wondered how Bobby and Ethel's daughter, a thoroughly competent young woman who was thought by some to be the most gifted Kennedy of her generation, responded to that notion.

I'll never forget the day in Hyannis Port when Mrs. Kennedy's stoic mask slipped for a moment and revealed the depth of her sorrow over losing those great men who were her sons. Mrs. Kennedy and her daughter Jean were talking about dinner that night, and Mrs. Kennedy inquired who was coming to join her. "I'll be here, and Eunice and Pat are coming, and so is Ethel." Her mother's obvious unresponsiveness led Jean to continue. "What more could you want?" she asked teasingly. In a low but carrying voice, Mrs. Kennedy uttered her desire, never before spoken but probably continually in her heart: "I want my sons."

That special feeling about sons expressed itself in many little ways. For example, Mrs. Kennedy, who had been giving away some of her more valuable possessions (both to make sure they were distributed the way she wanted them to be and to avoid heavy inheritance taxes for her children in the future), decided that Teddy should have the complete set of silver from the Palm Beach house. An ornate pattern adorned with a lion's head, it was not only worth a great deal of money (a complete service for twelve plus extra pieces such as a cocktail shaker and an ice bucket) but obviously carried precious memories. She tried to make her decision sound strictly logical; after all, his initial was "K," which was what was engraved on the silver. When someone brought up the fact that Ethel and all of her children had the same initial, Mrs. Kennedy abruptly changed the subject. Mrs. Kennedy later told Eunice that she wanted *her* to have an old English cream and sugar set, but it turned out that she expected her daughter to *buy* it. Eunice handed over a check for four thousand dollars without comment.

I could see why Mrs. Kennedy might take special pleasure

in making gifts to Teddy. Whatever his mother gave him—family photos, posters from World War II, a fifty-dollar check for Christmas—the Senator always appeared extremely grateful. Once when he came to lunch with her at Hyannis Port, she told me to run up to the attic and get a set of highball glasses we had found there. The glasses were nothing special, and they came with a plastic tray that would look out of place in any well-decorated home. Yet when I came into the room bearing this dubious gift, Ted showed nothing but happiness. "Maybe I could use this on the boat," he said, thanking her warmly. Perhaps that quality of appreciation on his part was why the tone of her letters to him seemed especially warm and loving. I remember a lovely note she slipped in with his Christmas check one year that mentioned her "heart full of love and appreciation for all you have done throughout the years."

It was impossible to tell whether her daughters ever resented this special treatment accorded their younger brother. Of all the "girls," Eunice was the one who seemed to be closest to her mother. They shared an interest in helping the retarded, and they were similarly energetic and determined women. Eunice's need to stay active every waking moment of her life struck me as nearly obsessive. I felt she was competing not really with others, but with something inside herself; it seemed as if she was trying to prove something to herself all the time. Perpetually on the go, she was demonstrably less domestic than the other women in the family. Her household simply ran itself, lurching along from one problem to the next. Turnover of staff at the Shrivers was high. Not only was she a very demanding employer, but a difficult one as well. I was told by one of her employees that Eunice had a way of giving everyone unsigned and therefore nonnegotiable paychecks just as she departed for a long trip. In the all-too-frequent periods when Eunice's house was understaffed, she or her daughter, Maria, often called Mrs. Kennedy's cook to ask her how to prepare something. One morning they phoned bright and early to find out how to cook bacon!

It was typical of Eunice that even though she didn't know much about cooking, she undauntedly set about preparing the family meal. Nothing fazed her. I remember the time in Florida when she was late getting dressed and the rest of the family left (in the only car) for mass without her. The unstoppable Eunice simply walked out on North Ocean Boulevard and waved at passing cars until one picked her up. This episode made the local paper, because in exclusive Palm Beach, hitchhikers are about as common as snowballs.

I always thought Eunice cared more for getting things accomplished than she did about the feelings of the people involved. Yet she was certainly an obedient daughter, and she was also a good mother. I did notice, though, that whenever Mrs. Kennedy wanted to discuss what she thought was a problem with one of the Shriver children, she addressed her note to Sarge rather than to Eunice. He was undoubtedly the head of that household.

If Eunice was Mrs. Kennedy's favorite daughter, she could also be the one to cause the most vexation. Mrs. Kennedy was constantly irritated by Eunice's sloppy glooming. "Eunice never did have any flair for clothes and she never cared about her appearance," she once complained. "I used to be ashamed of the way she looked. I was afraid people would think I neglected her." When Mrs. Kennedy went to Washington to attend a benefit for the retarded sponsored by President and Mrs. Ford, she came back shaking her head about the way Eunice had looked: She had lost the belt to her dress and never even noticed it was missing. When Sarge Shriver made his bid for the presidency in 1976, Mrs. Kennedy decided she had better help Eunice pick out clothes for the campaign. She came back from her shopping trip in the fall of 1975 with practically nothing for herself. "Like a dumb bunny, I spent all my time helping Eunice," she explained. Another time when she was passing through New York, she stopped into Bergdorf Goodman and picked out something she thought would be suitable and had it sent to Eunice. As it turned out, this caused a flap when her other daughters found out about it. In the end, she had to buy them new dresses, too.

Eunice often acted without thinking about the problems

she would cause other people. If she passed through Mrs. Kennedy's kitchen and spotted a freshly baked cake, she would simply dig out a handful for an instant snack. If she was having dinner guests at her own house in Hyannis Port, she would drop by her mother's and help herself to the carefully arranged vase of flowers on the dining room table (much to the annoyance of Jeannette, who had done the work of arranging them). She would call to ask Mrs. Kennedy's staff for all sorts of services: searching for a pair of missing earrings (later found in her own house), ordering me to send her a small package by air express, and similar chores.

These requests were usually accompanied by the injunction "Don't tell Mother." But sometimes it was impossible to hide such things from Mrs. Kennedy's vigilant attention. Once, for example, Eunice called me to ask for the number of the Senator's Washington office, and it just happened that I took the call in Mrs. Kennedy's bedroom, where we were working together. Of course she overheard the conversation, and the result was a reprimand to Eunice. Mrs. Kennedy paid my salary, and she wanted no one else to encroach on my time. The strangest part about this episode was the fact that Eunice got furious at me because she concluded I had "tattled" to her mother. For weeks afterward, whenever I happened to bump into her doing something around Mrs. Kennedy's house, she would say sarcastically, "I suppose you're going to tell Mother all about this."

Pat and Jean seemed to have a more placid relationship with their mother. She did criticize both of them for their drinking, although she didn't realize the extent of it until she began to read hints in the newspapers. Mrs. Kennedy herself never drank, and she was opposed to drinking on principle: "I think it's stupid," she said emphatically. She once told me, "My husband used to say I was terrible because he made a lot of money from liquor and I never drank any." She considered the purchase of liquor an unnessary expense, and moreover she was convinced that if she kept liquor in the house, the staff would drink it right up. So generally her daughters had to bring their own supply, creating a situation in which drinking took on the character of a secret and solitary vice. Various members of the family would keep their favorite wines in their rooms when they came to visit. Characteristically, an exception was made for Teddy. When he came to Palm Beach, I was always sent out to the liquor store to get some rum so he could mix up his renowned daiquiris. Everyone in the family loved them. So much so that the first time I was sent on that errand, I failed to buy enough rum; the Senator ran out by lunchtime on Sunday and had to ask a favorite restaurant to open up and sell him a bottle.

Pat, the only member of the family without a summer home on the Atlantic coast, was a frequent houseguest in Hyannis Port and in Palm Beach as well. Like Eunice, she was capable of being a demanding guest, deputizing staff members to take care of errands and asking for favors such as picking up a copy of a best-seller and sending it to her air express. Once when I went to meet her at the airport, she arrived with only one bag, but a very heavy one. I offered to get her a porter, but she curtly refused. As she picked up the bag, I said dubiously, "That looks very heavy." She snapped, "It is! I thought you were going to help."

Her personality was a moody one, and she could be very determined about getting her way. On one occasion she and Eunice were planning to go to Boston together, and when her sister was a few minutes late, Pat simply drove off without her, much to Eunice's dismay.

The quietest member of the family was Jean Smith. For the most part, Jean seemed to go her own way. And since the Smiths had sold their summer house in Hyannis Port and bought one in New York, none of the family appeared very frequently. Like everyone else, Jean did come for Mrs. Kennedy's birthday in July and the big get-together over the Labor Day weekend that amounted to an annual family reunion. I happened to overhear an unsettling interchange between Jean and her mother on the subject of Jean's childhood as we were all swimming in the Palm Beach pool. Jean remarked, "I was shuffled off to boarding school at the age of eight," and Mrs. Kennedy replied somewhat defensively, "Well, what was I to do? Your father was always gone, or we were having dinners at the embassy or attending formal affairs. I had no time to spend with you children." Jean ended the conversation almost casually by saying, "That's why I'm still trying to get my head on straight." Her words made Mrs. Kennedy furious. She sputtered and stammered and then got right out of the pool. Even hours later, I could tell she was still nettled by her daughter's remark.

Mrs. Kennedy's maternal sensitivity to the slightest hint that her children had turned out anything but perfect made me understand why the thought of Rosemary, her retarded daughter, still caused her such torment. Rosemary lived under the meticulous care of the nuns at St. Coletta's in Wisconsin. From the time she went there in late 1941 until the summer of 1974, when I started working for Mrs. Kennedy, she had never left the vicinity of the convent. Mrs. Kennedy told me she visited Rosemary every year, and she had always wanted Rosemary to come home for a visit. But the Ambassador disapproved, on the grounds that it would be too upsetting for all concerned. It was not until five years after Joe Kennedy's death that his widow decided to do as *she* thought best. Rosemary came to the Cape in August.

She was the oldest surviving member of her generation— at that time in her fifties, although she looked much younger, with only a few strands of gray in her short curly hair. Tall and somewhat heavy, she was still pretty. Scanning the collection of family photos on display in the sun-room, I always thought the young Rosemary was the prettiest of all the girls, with a smooth, round face and very regular features. She was good-humored, and she generally liked to be around people. She had trouble with my name and ended up calling me "Arbarb," but she invariably greeted me with a smile. So pretty and agreeable—and heart-wrenching.

Rosemary's original mild retardation had been severely complicated by the results of the lobotomy she had undergone in 1941, when her usually agreeable temperament began to show signs of deterioration. Mrs. Kennedy told me that while she was away from home, her husband had authorized the performance of the operation in the belief that it would calm Rosemary down. The unfortunate results were not only a dramatic increase in her retardation but also a mild paralysis of her right side; she dragged that foot and had trouble controlling her hand. Of course the Kennedys had been heartsick over this turn of events, and Mrs. Kennedy was particularly upset by the loss of all the things she had slowly and painstakingly taught Rosemary to do. "I was so provoked. After all my work . . . she was even presented at Court . . . and she was reading and writing and showing so much improvement." Mrs. Kennedy had even gone to the trouble of learning to print her own letters instead of using script so they would be easy for Rosemary to read. But all that was beyond her reach now. . . . In all the years I worked for her, I never heard Mrs. Kennedy question her husband's judgment about anything, but I speculated about whether she sometimes blamed him for Rosemary's condition. Of course he had done all he could to provide for her financially. There was money in trust to guarantee good care all her life. At the convent she had her own house and her own car so she could be taken on outings. She even had a mink coat, to ward off the chill of the Wisconsin winters.

During Rosemary's visit, Mrs. Kennedy seemed virtually haunted by thoughts of her daughter. If we were working in her bedroom, she would suddenly get up and peer out the window that overlooked the sweeping lawn, hoping (or fearing?) to catch sight of Rosemary. In the middle of dictation, she would get up and walk to the window. "Where is Rosemary now?" she asked herself. After a long pause, she would murmur, "The poor little thing. . . ." One day when Mrs. Kennedy and I were swimming in the pool, the nuns brought Rosemary out, too. But she simply sat in one of the chairs at the side, not even glancing in our direction. Mrs. Kennedy gazed at her daughter for a long time, and for once her sorrow was plainly visible. At last she sighed, "Oh, Rosie, what have we done to you?"

Mrs. Kennedy constantly tried to elicit some sign of affection from her daughter. She spent time with her, and she did her best to make her happy. One day when the two of them were waiting for lunch to be served, Mrs. Kennedy settled Rosemary on the living room sofa and went herself to the piano, sitting on the bench covered by her mother's old needlepoint. She began to play some of her old favorites in the hope of soothing Rosemary. But her daughter reacted restlessly to this form of communication, and Mrs. Kennedy finally had to give up the attempt. Often Rosemary deliberately turned away from her mother, and occasionally she even lashed out at her in anger and hostility. One of the nuns told me that Rosemary couldn't forget how her mother tried to push her to keep up with the others when they were children and that she still felt resentful. I felt so sorry for Mrs. Kennedy, who simply would not stop trying to make some loving contact with her daughter. Perhaps this was especially important to her because of her awareness of some of the costs of her focus on Rosemary. She said in a letter to Ethel and Bobby's daughter Courtney that she felt she had neglected Jack because she was so frustrated and disconcerted by his younger sister Rosemary's insoluble problems.

The visit seemed hard on them both . . . maybe Joe Kennedy had been right after all. Rosemary was obviously bewildered by the change in her normal schedule and at times seemed virtually exhausted by the demands placed on her. One of the nuns said as they left, "Rosemary is very tired. She's not used to all this activity. She lives a very quiet life at the convent." The house itself had an upsetting effect. One day I heard her muttering "Kathleen" over and over; being in Hyannis Port again must have reawakened many memories of the long-dead sister who was closest to her in age.

Mrs. Kennedy's other children did their share to make Rosemary's visit a good one. The Senator took her and the nuns out on his big boat for the afternoon. And Eunice was wonderful with Rosemary. The way she talked to her was perfectly natural and easy. She never sounded condescending or acted like she was talking to a child. Of course, Eunice had experience with the retarded. She didn't just work for the cause; she became personally involved. And, like her mother, she had been a faithful visitor to the convent in Wisconsin, so the sisters had forged some sort of relationship. Kennedy-like, Eunice tended to plan a full day of activities for Rosemary, including swimming and sailing, but I think Rosemary was often frightened by these experiences, especially since her physical disability made them difficult for her. But Eunice, sure the exercise would be good for her, always insisted.

Over the next few years, Rosemary's visits finally became routine: a winter visit to Palm Beach and a summer visit to Hyannis Port. She was accompanied by two nuns because she required constant attention. She was very likely to wander off, especially if she saw a child. Eunice once tried to take her shopping and lost her in a department store—an event that was quickly picked up by the newspapers. Rosemary was always the subject of media interest. There were constant requests for stories about her, and one journalist even wrote to ask for an interview with Rosemary herself. A photographer in Palm Beach did succeed in getting pictures of Rosemary, and much to Mrs. Kennedy's distress, they were published in the *National Enquirer*.

Each of Rosemary's subsequent visits was just as traumatic for Mrs. Kennedy as the first. Tense and strained while her daughter was there, she nevertheless drove herself to spend as much time with Rosemary as possible, even insisting on going to the airport and sitting with her indifferent daughter in the VIP lounge until her plane began boarding. Mrs. Kennedy invariably became sick for days afterward and often had to stay in bed to regain her strength. She had severe headaches and her stomach was badly upset. The doctor who was called in during one of these inevitable collapses said plainly that he thought Rosemary's visits were simply too much for her and ought to be stopped. I agreed with him, because the toll they took on her was so obvious.

I would have liked to enlist the aid of Mrs. Kennedy's children to do something about the situation, but I had by that time already learned that they were not likely to help. It wasn't, of course, that they didn't care about their mother's welfare. Rather it was that they remained unable to alter the relationship that had existed since they were small children. Their mother was the one who told them what to do, not vice versa.

My first realization that Mrs. Kennedy's children would be of no help in getting her to look after herself came in the affair of the stair railing. In the Palm Beach house, the curving front staircase that rose from the foyer to the second floor was made of stone, with a stone wall as well, and the rather steep stairs had no railing. This worried me for Mrs. Kennedy's sake. She sometimes wandered around the house late at night without adequate illumination, and she often wore floppy slippers and long pajama bottoms (the elastic at the waist kept wearing out) that could trip her up. At her age, even a short fall down those treacherous stone stairs could be a serious matter. My concern doubled when I happened to notice deep grooves in the stone wall by the bend of the staircase—the marks left after years of Mrs. Kennedy's trying to dig her nails into the hard stone for support.

The obvious solution was a railing that she could hang on to while walking down the stairs. I discovered an attractive wrought-iron type, in keeping with the Spanish interior of the house, that could be installed for only a hundred dollars, and the New York office gave me the okay to have it done. But, of course, Mrs. Kennedy would have to be told that we proposed to spend the money. Although many expenditures were made without her knowledge, the whole point of installing a railing was for her to notice—and use—it. As I feared, she agreed in principle that a railing would be a good idea but balked at the cost. Since we seemed to be at an impasse, I decided to appeal to the Senator for help.

He was due to spend a weekend in Palm Beach soon, I knew. So I telephoned his Washington office and spoke to his secretary, the ever-reliable Angelique. Would she slip a note to the Senator as he left for the visit? Just explain the situation and ask him to try to persuade Mrs. Kennedy to install the railing. It seemed like a reasonable request, but I saw when he arrived that he was not planning to get involved. He had come down for a vacation, not an argument with his mother. The first time we were in the same room together, he gave me his coldest stare, as if daring me to raise the disagreeable subject. Needless to say, the railing was not discussed . . . and when I left years later, Mrs. Kennedy was still walking up and down those steep stone stairs with nothing to hold on to.

Some months later, I tried once again to enlist the Senator's aid in looking after his mother. This time it was in regard to Mrs. Kennedy's consumption of sleeping pills. She took them when she had had an upsetting day or when she hadn't gotten enough exercise to make her physically tired at night. The problem was that, like many older people, she was not careful about how many she took or when she took them. The result was that sometimes she didn't wake up as usual the next morning. The maid and I would find her spread-eagle on the bed, and it sometimes took a frighteningly long time to rouse her. Even after she was up, she was only marginally functional for much of the rest of the day, sometimes stumbling when she walked and unable to carry on any extended conversation.

Another aspect of this situation that worried me was the variety of sleeping pills she had and might take. To begin with, she had about nine different doctors (in Boston, New York, Washington, and Florida) and they were all writing prescriptions without knowing what else she might be taking. But she had other sources of sleeping pills as well. Friends and family members picked them up for her whenever they traveled to countries (Switzerland, for example) where they were sold over the counter rather than by prescription. I remember one time when Sarge called to be sure that Mrs. Kennedy had received the fifty sleeping pills he had bought her in Switzerland and sent to the house with thirteen-year-old Anthony Shriver. It seemed to me that at the very least, *one* of Mrs. Kennedy's doctors ought to be aware of all the medication she was taking, so he could check them for side effects or interactions that might be harmful. Such a step seemed rational; after all, she was a frail woman in her eighties who had recently had a stroke. Moreover, it was obvious that someone needed to talk to her about the dangers of these pills and alert her to be more careful with them.

I first attempted this mission myself. One summer morning in Hyannis Port, Jeannette and I once again discovered Mrs. Kennedy unable to get up because of the effects of her pills. Together, we finally managed to get her up and dressed, and then I walked her back and forth on the wide front porch overlooking the ocean for more than an hour. During this period, I screwed up my courage and told her it was dangerous for her to take pills like that. She said challengingly, "How do you know so much about it?" I couldn't help being amused: Here she was, groggy and still disoriented, yet she was just as scrappy as ever! I told her somewhat weakly that I had read a lot about it, but I could see her skepticism about this secondhand expertise. So I switched the ground of my argument and told her to think about what the press would say if something were to happen . . . the headlines would scream that Rose Kennedy took an overdose of sleeping pills. She responded immediately. "Yes, yes, you're right about that." For a time, she was more careful. But eventually she became forgetful again.

I wrote a personal note to the Senator explaining the reasons for my concern. I received a lovely note from him in return saying, "I appreciate your letter and I just wanted you to know that I'm giving it some thought and will be back in touch with you." But, in fact, I never heard from him further about the matter.

Instead, not long after, I received a call from Eunice, whom the Senator had apparently gone to about the problem. She said she hoped I would not get discouraged and that the family appreciated all I was trying to do. But she avoided the central question of what to do to help Mrs. Kennedy be more careful about taking sleeping pills. The next link in this chain of events was a conversation with Pat Lawford, who told me that in the future I was not to bother the Senator about Mrs. Kennedy's problems; from now on, she, Pat, would be in charge of the situation. By this time, however, I was not the least bit surprised that Pat had no intention of confronting Mrs. Kennedy on the subject either. When I brought it up, she simply shrugged and said, "No problem." On one occasion, when I pressed her tactlessly, she said, with a note in her voice that sounded virtually helpless, "There's nothing anyone can do. Once Mother makes up her mind about something, that's it."

Finally, after another groggy morning, I did get results. Jean Smith called and instructed me to go immediately into Mrs. Kennedy's bathroom, collect all the sleeping pills, and flush them down the toilet. "But don't tell Mother," she warned. Of course, I was all in favor of the idea, but I have to admit that as I crept into Mrs. Kennedy's bathroom while she ate lunch downstairs, I was just plain scared. I could all too easily imagine her expression if she happened to come in and find me at work. In a way, my pounding heart made me part of the family, as I, too, was hesitant to incur Mrs. Kennedy's wrath.

After her lunch, Mrs. Kennedy went upstairs for her nap. A few minutes later, she walked down the hall to my office and asked if I knew anything about her missing sleeping pills. I could only lie, saying, "Oh, no, Mrs. Kennedy." About half an hour later, she was back. "Are you sure you don't know anything about my sleeping pills?" she demanded. I saw that as usual it was going to be impossible to deceive her, so I admitted the truth. "Everyone was very concerned about you, Mrs. Kennedy," I explained. She tossed her head angrily. "Hmfph! How can they do this to me, treating me just like a child!" Even at her age, she was set on her independence. She went back to her bedroom, and immediately the light on one of the phone lines went on; it was easy to guess she was calling the children to give them a piece of her mind. As it happened, she couldn't reach anyone at that time. And after a few days, the whole thing blew over. Later I found out why Mrs. Kennedy forgot the matter so quickly: She had a secret cache of pills in her traveling case and was still getting into them. As usual, she had defeated all of us.

She did it again over the issue of her stomach problems. Her stomach was very easily upset. It seemed like all the emotions she managed to refrain from displaying in any other way went right to her digestive system. Then she would be unable to eat even her usual bland diet and suffered discomfort that could keep her in bed for several days. She once told me she was sure she had ruined her stomach by the decades of rigorous dieting it had required to keep her slim, youthful figure. By the time I knew her, she had for years been unable to eat anything but simple dishes such as baked chicken, custard, and pureed vegetables. No salads, no spices, as little fat as possible, luke-warm beverages, meals eaten at precisely the same time every day: She was a slave to her stomach. Her only weakness was dessert, and especially a crisp sugar cookie made from a favorite recipe in *The Fannie Farmer Cookbook*. In both Palm Beach and Hyannis Port, the cook saw to it that there was always a fresh batch in the cookie jar, and Mrs. Kennedy helped herself whenever she walked through the kitchen. During one restless night, she managed to eat every cookie in the jar—all thirty-three of them! This may have been the occasion on which she made the discovery that there were always crumbs at the bottom of the jar that she hated to see going to waste. The next day, she ordered the cook to serve her the crumbs in a little bowl, and I have to confess I couldn't resist the temptation of walking by the dining room to see what she was going to do with them. She neatly solved the problem by pouring them over her usual dish of custard as a sort of crunchy topping.

But such binges were rare. It was more common to find her unable to take any interest in her food and suffering from painful stomach cramps and diarrhea. She had some medicine that she occasionally took at such times, but it had been pre-scribed many years ago, and her condition seemed to be growing worse. The obvious solution would be to see a doctor about the problem, but apparently that was one of the things Mrs. Kennedy had made up her mind not to do.

So the children resorted to a stratagem that was as comic as it was ineffective. When the Senator came down to Palm Beach one weekend that spring, he and Eunice invited Mrs. Kennedy's New York doctor, also in Palm Beach on a holiday, for cocktails one evening. He was supposed to observe her dis-creetly and then perhaps engage her in conversation about her ailment. Then, according to their scenario, he would make a diagnosis and prescribe medication that would be more effective. Since I wasn't at the cocktail gathering, I don't know exactly how Mrs. Kennedy managed to elude the doctor's scrutiny: whether she was uncomfortably aware of his interest and gave him a wide berth, or guessed at the plot that had been laid, or simply didn't find the man interesting enough to bother with. Whatever the reason, the doctor failed miserably in his mission and Mrs. Kennedy went along as before, having occasional bad spells with her stomach.

Another failure came when I brought up the problem of Mrs. Kennedy's long walks. She generally went out for an hour or more in the afternoon, but if she couldn't sleep, she might decide to have another stroll at ten or eleven at night. Since both her sight and her hearing were failing, I worried that she might lose her way. And what if she felt ill when she was out alone somewhere? Once she gave us a real fright in Hyannis Port when she went out for a walk on a rainy night that suddenly turned into a classic nor'easter. Jeannette called me at home around ten to say that Mrs. Kennedy had been out for nearly two hours and still hadn't returned. Beginning to imagine the worst, I called the police and rushed over to the house myself. Just as we were all working ourselves up, a vivacious (and thoroughly dry) Mrs. Kennedy appeared—in a car driven by thoughtful neighbors who had seen her sitting on their front porch to take shelter and had invited her in for a cup of hot tea. Needless to say, she was amused to find everyone so worried about her.

After that experience, I enlisted several of Ethel's younger children as a sort of makeshift patrol. Explaining my concern about their grandmother's habit of taking long walks at night, I asked if they could keep an eye on her without letting her know they were watching. Max, then about ten, was especially good about this, perhaps because he was just the right age to love engaging in such conspiracies. When she went out, he would trail her like a spy, lurking out of sight and concealing himself behind the bushes . . . heaven knows what the neighbors thought of it! Of course, it was no real solution to the long-term problem. But once again, Mrs. Kennedy's children, handicapped by their love and respect for their mother and perhaps most of all by their long tradition of obedience to parental command, were literally unable to intervene.

I could see that Mrs. Kennedy must certainly have been maddening at times to her family. About her children's affairs, she could be cool and critical. About her own, she was often headstrong and willful. Yet Mrs. Kennedy remained the center of her children's universe, just as they were hers. No family was ever bound together more tightly than the Kennedys.

4

The Magic Family

The time and energy that other women might spread out over careers and friendships and community service, Rose Kennedy concentrated entirely on her family. Her career *was* her family, and she ran it like the chief executive officer, with a CEO's concern for success. Her family also took the place of friends. Kennedys just naturally did things with other Kennedys, not outsiders. Even her charity work with the mentally retarded was merely an extension of her familial concern over Rosemary.

What journalists like to call "the Kennedy mystique" had become so strong that even the Kennedys themselves couldn't help but begin to believe in it. And much of that mystique emanated from the matriarch, Mrs. Kennedy. Ted might be the head of the family, but Mrs. Kennedy remained its symbol. She was the guardian of the traditions, the link to the past . . . no wonder the other Kennedys were always concerned about her opinion.

Like many people with roots in the nineteenth century, Mrs. Kennedy gave a broad definition to the concept of "family." It didn't mean just her children—although they were of course the first, the inner circle—but the entire web of relationships by blood and by marriage that had been created over three or

four generations. All of these connections were important ob-
ligations in Mrs. Kennedy's eyes.

She was certainly a formidable mother-in-law. She accepted
the husbands and wives of her children into the family, but she
expected them to behave like Kennedys. And she always felt
free to criticize . . . for someone's own good. For example, she
sent Ethel a little note just before the annual RFK tennis tour-
nament suggesting that she try to remember to stand up straight,
as her bad posture often spoiled her looks in published photographs. She criticized Eunice's grammar after she was quoted
as saying, "with whom I could not live without." Later she told
Pat to be sure to use her verbs correctly and went on to give
her two pages of examples, some of them rather bizarre: "The
girls struck the house." "The lightning struck us."

Mrs. Kennedy delighted in giving both daughters and
daughters-in-law "tips" about how to look their best in public.
Amusingly, much of this advice she had herself received from
England's Queen Elizabeth (the present Queen Mother). She
told the girls they should always wear a hat that doesn't conceal
the face; they should wear bright colors to stand out in the crowd;
and they should remember to pose for photographs with their
arms bent and held away from the body to create the illusion of
greater slimness. If you look at photos of Mrs. Kennedy in her
later years, you'll see she always bent her arms that way, even
when she was sitting. Jean Smith once said laughingly that as
far as she could see, the pose made you look as if your arm were
broken!

Mrs. Kennedy made a special effort to remain close to her
sons' widows, Ethel and Jackie. Of course, both of them had
summer houses next to hers in the Kennedy compound at Hyannis Port, so it was easy for her to see them frequently. I thought
Mrs. Kennedy always seemed particularly eager to please Jackie.

One reason for Mrs. Kennedy's attitude might have been
her genuine admiration for the way Jackie had withstood the
tragic events of her life. On one of the very rare occasions when
the subject of President Kennedy's assassination came up, Mrs.
Kennedy said to me, "I don't see how Jackie stood it, being

there and witnessing all that." She later expressed another aspect of her feelings for Jackie in a letter she wrote to Caroline at the time that Aristotle Onassis was gravely ill. She told Caroline that she felt so sorry for Jackie, since she had had so many trials in her life and was still so young. At the time of Jackie's marriage to Aristotle Onassis, in 1969, I read rumors that Mrs. Kennedy was very upset about it. But I discovered that in fact she was very supportive of Jackie's decision and seemed to understand some of the reasons behind it. She commented that she thought Onassis was a very charming man, but not at all attractive, and usually rather badly dressed in ill-fitting clothes, especially baggy trousers. She compared his physical appeal unfavorably with that of Lord Harlech, one of Jackie's earlier escorts, but added with wry understanding, "But then, of course, Lord Harlech didn't own private islands and yachts."

She always enjoyed the glamour of visits from Jackie and Ari, and she liked to tell the story of the time Onassis came to visit her in her New York apartment. When he arrived, he gave her a little box containing a gold bracelet with a snake's head outlined in red and white stones. She thanked him perfunctorily, assuming the bracelet was a piece of costume jewelry he had picked up in a nearby department store. Some years later, she sent it with some other pieces to be appraised and was startled to learn it contained real diamonds and rubies.

I suspect that Mrs. Kennedy was quite impressed by Jackie's good taste and innate elegance. One time when Jackie was sitting in the sun-room of Mrs. Kennedy's Hyannis Port house, she happened to remark on how much she liked the fabric of the curtains (a flowered chintz with a white background) and how appropriate it was for the setting. She casually added that it might look nice to have the sofa and armchairs covered in matching fabric. Her offhand comment generated an absolute frenzy of activity. Mrs. Kennedy summoned Bob Luddington, a decorator from Jordan Marsh in Boston who often helped her with the Hyannis Port house, and told him to buy more fabric and have slipcovers made. The only problem was that the curtains were ten years old and the fabric long since discontinued. It took Bob months, but eventually he tracked down enough of the fabric to carry out Mrs. Kennedy's orders. Then it turned out that the new fabric didn't exactly match the old curtains, since they had yellowed from a decade of hanging in the sun. Still, Jackie proved to be right, and the sun-room did look more cheerful and better coordinated once the new slipcovers were installed.

Mrs. Kennedy's desire to please Jackie was especially evident one evening when she was coming over for dinner. All day long, everyone was running around at top speed, fixing the floral arrangements and digging up some special linen place mats Mrs. Kennedy wanted to use. There was much discussion of the menu, and the cook outdid herself with *boeuf à la mode*, a splendid roast made the real French way, soaked in red wine, enriched with a good veal glaze, and finished with flaming brandy. Dessert was a light but flavorful coffee mousse, substituting Sanka so Mrs. Kennedy (who rigorously avoided caffeine because it upset her stomach) could have some, too. After the meal, Jackie complimented the cook: "Oh, Nellie, you could go out there and take a leaf from one of those trees and turn it into something fabulous!" Such comments made it clear why everyone tried so hard to please her.

I was always impressed by Jackie's tactful way of dealing with Mrs. Kennedy. For example, during the several years that Mrs. Kennedy was virtually obsessed with cleaning out the attic in Hyannis Port, she kept pressing on Jackie things she found there. Some red glass vases, for example, quite obviously didn't match the cranberry glass that Jackie had painstakingly collected over the years, but Jackie graciously accepted them and thanked Mrs. Kennedy with great courtesy. Later Mrs. Kennedy found a pair of antique tin reflectors, the kind that were once placed behind candles, and wanted to sell them to her daughter-in-law. Jackie quietly paid the $170 Mrs. Kennedy asked for, even though with her connoisseur's eye she had noticed that the reflectors were damaged and thus virtually worthless as antiques. "I'm only buying those broken reflectors to make her happy," she explained. Once, when I went to Jackie's house to deliver some-

56

thing else Mrs. Kennedy wanted her to have, I said, "I guess you can put it in *your* attic." Jackie laughed and answered, "Oh, that's all right. I like old attics full of things to go through."

Jackie's gifts to Mrs. Kennedy were always very thoughtfully chosen: a huge white poinsettia to decorate the Palm Beach living room for Christmas, luxurious sheets hand-embroidered to match the color of Mrs. Kennedy's bedroom decor, an ornate silver cross she brought back from one of the Greek islands. In turn, Mrs. Kennedy often spent more time and thought on presents for Jackie than she did for most other members of the family.

Mrs. Kennedy usually dispatched her Christmas shopping quickly and easily by calling Elizabeth Arden's, on exclusive Worth Avenue in Palm Beach, and ordering a sweater sent to each daughter and daughter-in-law. But she was willing to spend more time looking for just the right thing for Jackie. One year she and I browsed in Courrèges, and she was on the verge of buying a simple white pullover to give Jackie for Christmas until she found out it would cost seventy-five dollars. "I'm not spending that much money," she said loudly, and made a quick exit. I was especially surprised by her change of heart because she was so fond of Jackie. But she clearly felt that particular sweater was overpriced. In any case, whatever Mrs. Kennedy finally selected, Jackie was always prompt and graceful in her thanks. She was a good correspondent, and Mrs. Kennedy liked to save her letters. I found notes Jackie had written from on board the Onassis yacht, the *Christina*, on the elegant pale blue stationery provided for all passengers, and short letters describing a particular event, often addressing Mrs. Kennedy as Grand-mère rather than Gramma. I even found a letter that Jackie had written to the Kennedys when she and Jack were on their honeymoon in Acapulco, full of amusing anecdotes: Jack catching a big sailfish, his efforts to speak Spanish, her initial difficulty in learning to water-ski. That letter left no doubt about the fact that Jackie had been very much in love with her husband.

I thought another reason that Mrs. Kennedy had a good relationship with Jackie was that she and her children kept pretty much to themselves. Despite the fact that Jackie's house in

Hyannis Port bordered Mrs. Kennedy's, they were rarely to be seen, and Jackie never visited in Palm Beach the entire time I worked for Mrs. Kennedy. She dutifully put in an appearance at Mrs. Kennedy's birthday party and the big Labor Day family get-together, and she sometimes formally invited Mrs. Kennedy to dinner and accepted similarly formal return invitations. But for the most part, Jackie went her own way, and thus she and her household remained a kind of special treat to Mrs. Kennedy.

Ethel and her family, on the other hand, were constantly visible. Mrs. Kennedy had only to look out her dining room window or step out on her big porch to see everything that was going on next door at Ethel's house in Hyannis Port. Perhaps their relationship had more of the strains common to all close families.

Like most mothers-in-law who come into close contact with their daughters-in-law, Mrs. Kennedy was sometimes disapproving in her comments about Ethel. One of her favorite targets of criticism was what she called "Ethel's extravagance." When I once commented how the smell of Ethel's perfume remained in the house long after she had gone, Mrs. Kennedy remarked drily, "The rest of us buy French perfume by the ounce; Ethel buys it by the quart." (In all seriousness, though, Ethel's heavy scent did seem to bother Mrs. Kennedy because she switched from her long-time favorite by Guerlain when Ethel started using it.)

Ethel was quite knowledgeable about vintage wine and ordered her favorite Pouilly Fuissé by the case. She bought expensive leather belts by the half dozen, and when she liked a designer dress, she often ordered it in two or three colors. The food served at her house was always abundant and usually very luxurious—lobster tails, prime ribs of beef, and other gourmet goodies, served to even the youngest children. One night when Mrs. Kennedy was invited to Ethel's for dinner, she asked me what the menu was. I told her it would be Alaskan king crab, rice pilaf, and spinach soufflé. In a tone of mock awe, she responded, "Oh, my, what it is to be rich!"

More disturbing to Mrs. Kennedy than Ethel's extravagance

was what seemed like her failure to discipline her children properly. To be fair, the task of bringing up eleven fatherless children could overwhelm anyone. Moreover, the free and easy atmosphere of Ethel's home attracted all the other grandchildren, so disturbances originating in her house were not necessarily instigated by Ethel's children. But they did seem to be a noisy bunch, and they might be found anywhere—playing on Mrs. Kennedy's lawn, running on the beach or frolicking in the water, crashing around their own front porch, or even climbing on the roof of their house. It was just the sort of behavior to worry an elderly lady of settled habits who had a natural concern for her grandchildren's safety. Every summer, there would be a barrage of notes and phone calls to Ethel's household about problems caused by the children. Mrs. Kennedy once commented that she thought it was a shame the way things had turned out, after they had conceived all those children. But Bobby and Ethel were so crazy about one another. . . .

It seemed to me that Ethel tried hard to be considerate of Mrs. Kennedy. She was always polite and accepted the rather frequent admonitions from her mother-in-law as gracefully as the circumstances made possible. She understood Mrs. Kennedy's dedication to her regular routine and tried not to upset it. When she was a visitor in Palm Beach, she came prepared to fit right in; understanding that it would be difficult to keep her bathroom cleaned because of the usual shortage of staff, she simply asked for the necessary supplies to do it herself. Unlike most of "the children," she didn't make demands on Mrs. Kennedy's staff, and she was always especially nice to me, so I've always thought of her fondly. And she was considerate of her mother-in-law in small ways. She was the one who noticed (one day in church) that the good costume pearls Mrs. Kennedy usually wore were dirty, and she gave her a new strand; Mrs. Kennedy thanked Ethel in a warm letter that praised her for being wonderfully thoughtful. Ethel frequently invited Mrs. Kennedy over for dinner or sent her famous houseguests over to make a call on her . . . whatever might help make her mother-in-law a little less lonely.

I sometimes wondered if Mrs. Kennedy didn't also share a typical mother-in-law's jealousy of her daughter-in-law's relationship with Bobby. For instance, the one time the supposed affair between Bobby and Marilyn Monroe came up, Mrs. Kennedy said to me, "I don't believe it could have happened . . . Bobby was always so *sanctimonious*." It sounded almost as if she held it against him that he didn't have the roving eye so characteristic of the other men in the family.

For her part, Ethel remained devoted to Bobby's memory. She still wore his engagement ring and wedding band, and even when she traveled, a picture of Bobby in a silver frame was always on the table beside her bed. Yet according to one of the household staff, Ethel had angered Mrs. Kennedy the previous winter when she visited in Palm Beach and had dates with an unidentified "boyfriend," even going so far as kissing him when they were together at the house. I always doubted the gossip, because surely Mrs. Kennedy knew no one could ever take Bobby's place for Ethel. I remember one time when we were discussing Ethel and her children, and I said sympathetically, "She needs a man around, Mrs. Kennedy." She responded, "Don't we all!"

For me, Mrs. Kennedy's attitude toward Ethel was best summed up by a remark I happened to hear her make to herself. She was looking out the window at the scene at the house next door: children running and shouting, toys strewn all over the lawn, no responsible adult in sight. She turned away with a sigh and said almost angrily, "I don't know what Bobby meant by going away and leaving Ethel with all those children to raise alone."

Mrs. Kennedy's attitude toward her youngest daughter-in-law, Joan, was more puzzled than censorious. By the mid-1970s, Joan's drinking problem had become obvious, and Mrs. Kennedy was quite aware of it. Once, when Joan turned up in Palm Beach unexpectedly, taking a bus from Cocoa Beach where she had been visiting her mother, Mrs. Kennedy went into her bedroom to greet her. When she came back down the hall, she rolled her eyes, tossed her head, and said disdainfully, "Oh, *baby*!" In fact,

Joan, who had been in the house only a few hours, was already packing to return to Washington. Shortly after her arrival, Teddy had telephoned and apparently read her the riot act, for she left as suddenly as she had arrived. On another of Joan's visits, Mrs. Kennedy must have decided to try physical therapy. Before poor Joan could even unpack, she was sent to the library to sort through the dusty volumes looking for signed first editions that might be valuable. She gamely stayed at this dirty and difficult task all afternoon and then shut herself up in her bedroom until the middle of the next day. (She and her husband had separate rooms, a fact I knew Mrs. Kennedy was unhappy about.) On another visit, Joan was assigned the task of checking the condition of all the lampshades in the house, so Mrs. Kennedy could replace the oldest and shabbiest of them.

It must have been unpleasant for Joan, the way people were always watching her. Whenever her husband saw her, he seemed to be peering at her intently, as if trying to ascertain her condition. And the rest of the family acted the same way. She attracted all this attention, even though she wasn't the only person in the family who ever drank too much. And she generally behaved herself perfectly well. Drunk or sober, she was always soft-spoken and ladylike. In some ways, she seemed more genuinely concerned about Mrs. Kennedy than anyone else in the family—or at least more observant. On one of her visits, she made the comment to me that she saw that Mrs. Kennedy was not really "with it" much of the time, and she intended to speak to Ted about it.

At that time in her life, Joan simply seemed to me like a victim of fate. Perhaps Mrs. Kennedy had the same feelings, for she didn't really criticize Joan. Instead, she tried to understand what was wrong. According to her viewpoint, Joan had everything: good looks, a handsome husband, two lovely homes, her own secretary, and three attractive children. If the marriage wasn't perfect, and the pressures of fame were sometimes very great . . . well, those were just things you had to learn to bear. Mrs. Kennedy herself had borne as much, or more. She had long ago adopted a philosophy of consciously trying her best to be happy, no matter what the circumstances, and this philo-sophic commitment was supported by her deep belief in God's goodness and His ultimate purpose. Rose Kennedy refused to consider her own marriage an unhappy one, although (to judge from published reports) there must surely have been periods in its fifty-five-year duration when she felt neglected, even be-trayed. But she did her best to focus on only the good things: the beautiful homes, the achievements of the family, the comfort and security of wealth, the opportunity to travel and meet world-famous people. Her own attitude made Mrs. Kennedy literally unable to understand why Joan was suffering. But she tried. She treated her daughter-in-law kindly, spoke of her politely—but never truly could empathize with her, despite her efforts.

Mrs. Kennedy's relationships with her sons-in-law were even more distant. By the time I worked for Mrs. Kennedy, Pat had divorced her actor husband, Peter Lawford, so he never came to Mrs. Kennedy's.

Jean's husband, Steve, also stayed outside Mrs. Kennedy's orbit. Although Steve Smith ran the office in New York that handled the financial affairs of the entire Kennedy family, he had little contact with the matriarch of the clan. I remember that he came once to Palm Beach with Jean and the children. He was scheduled to fly to New York for a few days of business and then return to Florida to finish out the vacation with his family. But just as he was leaving for New York, Mrs. Kennedy asked him—politely but firmly—not to return to Florida, be-cause the house was already overcrowded. That was the last we ever saw of Steve Smith.

I found his absence a little strange, in light of the fact that he was so important to the family as a financial manager and general troubleshooter. He was an influential voice in the family meetings when the assembled "elders" discussed things like where the grandchildren should be sent for the summer and whether Mrs. Kennedy ought to live with one of the children. He was called in when a child was in trouble or when legal problems loomed. For example, he made a trip out West to get Ethel out of a lawsuit brought by a caterer when she refused to pay his bill for a party she had given. He hired an attorney and straightened the matter out for her—and then, when he was ready to return to the East Coast, Ethel told him there wasn't room for him on her private plane, so he had to take a commercial flight. Perhaps it was this sort of experience that had taught him not to expect much in the way of gratitude from the Kennedys. I understood he told someone in the New York office that he was just waiting for the day when one of the grandchildren sued him for mismanaging the family funds.

Sarge Shriver was the son-in-law who had the most contact with Mrs. Kennedy. He and Eunice had their own house in Hyannis Port, and he often accompanied his family when they went to visit Mrs. Kennedy in Palm Beach. Sarge came from a well-to-do family and knew how the "old rich" lived, which was emphatically not the way Mrs. Kennedy did things at this period in her life. (Mrs. Kennedy once said of Sarge, "Blue blood, no money.") Mrs. Kennedy's eccentric economies always seemed to pain him. He reminded me of the princess in the fairy tale who was so thoroughly royal that she could feel a single pea through the thickness of a hundred mattresses. Although he knew perfectly well that there was only one domestic in the entire Palm Beach house, he persisted in expecting services possible only from a large staff. For example, one time (after he had just announced himself to be a presidential candidate) he asked me to see that his shoes were polished—as if we had a bootblack hidden away in the back of the house! I ended up taking them to a shoe repair shop to be polished. When Mrs. Kennedy learned that the bill for this service would be $1.50, she was very disapproving of such extravagance.

Sarge certainly could be lavish with other people's money. He was the one who talked Mrs. Kennedy into trading her Chrysler New Yorker in for a more expensive Lincoln Continental. Someone in the New York office commented about that, saying, "Sarge doesn't have two dimes to rub together, but he sure can spend other people's money." And he would casually order hundreds of dollars' worth of food and liquor in Palm Beach, to be charged to Mrs. Kennedy's account. But to give him credit, he wasn't stingy with his own money either. He would spend just as freely when he was the one picking up the tab.

One almost comical afternoon epitomized for me the difference between Sarge's accustomed ways of doing things and the way Mrs. Kennedy liked to run her household. In an outburst of hospitality during the Christmas holidays, Mrs. Kennedy had invited visiting socialite Gloria Guinness to stop in for a cup of tea at the end of her afternoon of shopping on Worth Avenue. She then asked her son-in-law Sarge to take charge of organizing the hospitality for this rare occasion.

Of course, there was as usual no liquor in the house, so Sarge came charging into my office a little before 5:00 P.M. to tell me to arrange to get something to drink. As it happened, I was helping a friend throw a party that night and with Mrs. Kennedy's permission was planning to leave fifteen minutes early. In fact, I was actually in the process of changing my clothes when Sarge burst in. I explained that I was leaving, but gave him the number of a nearby liquor store that always delivered promptly. His initial response was to make a sarcastic query about the hours I was supposed to work. He went on to complain about how the rest of the staff (that meant a total of two people, one of them temporary) were no help either. Then he asked me where to find a tablecloth. I explained that there were none in the house. Since Eunice had earlier asked me to run an errand during my lunch hour and pick up a rental projector to show a film about her brother Jack, I assumed the tablecloth was to be used as a movie screen and suggested Sarge use a sheet instead. He got very huffy with me, but I felt it was hardly my fault that Mrs. Kennedy didn't have any tablecloths.

It was evident that Sarge had riled both the cook and the maid with his spate of demands, and I was afraid there was going to be a domestic explosion before the evening was over. Both servants were perfectly capable of simply walking out if they got too annoyed, so I thought perhaps I should mention the situation to Mrs. Kennedy before I left. I knocked on her bedroom door and she called, "Come in." I did . . . to find my employer wearing a very dressy pinwheel hat and absolutely nothing else! I found conversing with a nude employer rather distracting, so I just quickly explained to Mrs. Kennedy that Sarge seemed to be upsetting the entire staff and the consequences might be disastrous. "Oh, I can't be bothered with that now," she said, as she continued to adjust the hat she planned to wear for Mrs. Guinness's visit. I fled, leaving the entire matter in the hands of fate.

When I came to work the next morning, I discovered a makeshift bar set up at one end of the living room, on a table covered with a white bed sheet. I giggled when I tried to imagine what the coolly elegant Gloria Guinness must have thought about that arrangement! In my office, I found a sixty-five-dollar liquor bill on my desk. And in no time at all, the maid was in my office to tell me how Mrs. Guinness had refused everything except a cup of plain tea.

Later that morning, Sarge appeared in my office and said Mrs. Kennedy had told him he must apologize to me. The effect of the apology was definitely undercut by his next remark, which was to ask me what he had done. I told him he couldn't order Mrs. Kennedy's staff around the way he had been doing. The house was understaffed in the first place, and the pay Mrs. Kennedy offered was so low that I had trouble finding replacements when anyone left. My temper then got the best of me, I'm afraid, and I concluded by telling him that slavery had been abolished one hundred years ago. Actually, when I cooled down, I had to admit that Sarge was only trying to be helpful in his own way. It certainly was true that, with her small staff and tendency to entertain so infrequently, Mrs. Kennedy's hospitality was usually very hit-or-miss. He just never could get used to the limitations of Mrs. Kennedy's household.

I thought Sarge always tried hard to please Mrs. Kennedy. This was vividly demonstrated on an occasion when the Shrivers were visiting in Palm Beach as Mrs. Kennedy was preparing to make a short speech on some occasion on behalf of the retarded. Sarge—a former ambassador to France, running mate of George

McGovern on the Democratic ticket in 1972, and presidential hopeful in the upcoming 1976 election—volunteered to help his mother-in-law write her speech. He really worked hard, spending the whole sunny Florida afternoon shut up in the library, diligently writing and rewriting and even calling his sons in to listen to excerpts of his draft. At last, when Mrs. Kennedy woke up from her afternoon nap, he proudly handed her the finished product. She read it over and then asked me to look at it when I came to take dictation in her bedroom. I could tell she was dissatisfied, so when she asked me what I thought, I gave her my honest opinion. "It's a nice speech, Mrs. Kennedy, but it just doesn't sound like you." She nodded her head in agreement and walked over to the open bedroom door. In her most ladylike manner, she caroled out, "Oh, Sarge, dear, I'm afraid it won't do." An ominous silence emanated from the library down the hall, where he had been waiting for the verdict.

I got the impression that Mrs. Kennedy was lukewarm at best about Sarge's career as a politician. She did make a few appearances on his behalf, and she also gave him money to finance his campaign: to my knowledge, about $50,000. But she seemed to regard his political ambitions as a sort of expensive hobby. I remember I once boldly asked her why the Senator didn't come out and endorse his brother-in-law, and she replied airily, "Oh, he has good reasons." It was clear to me from her attitude that she thought her son was doing the right thing by remaining silent. After Sarge dropped out of the presidential race, there were rumors that he might run for governor of Maryland. Mrs. Kennedy said wryly, "I hope not. I'm getting sick and tired of making contributions to his campaigns."

Mrs. Kennedy's strong sense of family extended even to the families of her in-laws. When Joan's mother died, Mrs. Kennedy immediately arranged for a mass to be said for the repose of her soul. She also dispatched a warm telegram of condolence to Jackie's sister, Lee, on the death of her ex-husband, Prince Radziwell. She even maintained a little-publicized but quite strong connection with her daughter Kathleen's in-laws. I had read in many books that Mrs. Kennedy had been terribly opposed to her daughter's wartime marriage to the heir of the Duke of Devonshire because he was a staunch Protestant. Kathleen and Billy Cavendish met when the Kennedy family was in England during Joe's tenure as ambassador. Her father sent the whole family home when World War II broke out, but Kathleen missed her friends in England and soon joined the Red Cross so she could return. She and Billy dated for some time but hesitated to marry because of their religious affinities. Finally, love triumphed and they were married at a registry office during one of his brief leaves from the front. He was killed in action not long afterward. According to some writers, Mrs. Kennedy never forgave her daughter for marrying outside the Catholic Church, and they were still unreconciled when Kathleen was killed in a plane crash in 1948. Of course, I don't know what happened back in the 1940s, but I do know that all the time I was with Mrs. Kennedy she corresponded regularly and affectionately with Kathleen's former mother-in-law, now the Dowager Duchess of Devonshire. She addressed her by her nickname of "Moucher" and kept her up to date with all the Kennedy family news. The dowager duchess responded in the same vein. The connection extended to the next generation as well, for I recall that the present duke (the younger brother of Kathleen's husband) stopped off to see Mrs. Kennedy one time when he was in the States.

Then there was Mrs. Kennedy's own Fitzgerald family. Mrs. Kennedy was one of six children of onetime Boston mayor John F. Fitzgerald, and at the time I started to work for her, all three of her brothers were still living. There were also the nieces and nephews, and the grandnieces and grandnephews, and another generation to come. . . . The Fitzgeralds all seemed to me to be common, ordinary people despite the advantages of John Fitzgerald's political success and Rose's wealthy husband. One of her brothers had been a ticket-taker at the Mystic River Bridge in Boston. Dave Powers, a former aide to President Kennedy, liked to joke about how whenever Jack had to use that bridge, he would slide down in the backseat of the car to avoid notice by his uncle. Another Fitzgerald brother lived in a trailer somewhere in Maine.

It was Joe Kennedy who initiated the practice of providing for the education of the Fitzgerald nieces and nephews, and of course, he did the same for the children of his two younger sisters as well. He had financed the education of fourteen nieces and nephews, and at the time of his death, he was doing the same for the forty-three members of the next generation. According to gossip, Joe Kennedy had never been fond of the Fitzgerald relatives, but he felt an obligation to help them help themselves.

Mrs. Kennedy continued the tradition established by her husband. As the years went by, she grew more and more generous toward the Fitzgeralds. She gave each of her brothers a large annual check—$20,000 to $25,000. Mrs. Kennedy also sent each niece and nephew a Christmas check to put away for their own children's education. Originally, the amount had been $4,000 per child, but by the early 1970s she had, at the urging of the New York office, cut that back to $3,000. By 1976, she had decided to stop sending money after the children reached the age of twenty-one. The last year I worked for her, the New York office insisted on slashing the amount to $500. For families that had as many as seven children and were accustomed to receiving a check for over $20,000 each year, that came as a big surprise.

Part of the reason for the cutbacks was Mrs. Kennedy's concern about the way the relatives were using the money. As someone in the Kennedys' New York office told me, "These people are able to send their children to schools you and I could never afford, Barbara." The problem in Mrs. Kennedy's eyes was that the children were being sent to expensive private schools from the time they entered first grade. She was opposed to that idea, not only because of the expense but also because she thought it was good for children to rub up against all sorts of people. It had been a good learning experience for her own children to attend public school when they were young, and she thought the same principle would apply to the grandnieces and grand-nephews. She had been additionally distressed to discover that some of the children were not even going to college, despite all the money she had sent for their tuition.

Mrs. Kennedy once told me she thought she had given away at least $4 million to her relatives. Whatever the actual amount, it was certainly enough to disgruntle her children. One time when we were making the arrangements for one of Mrs. Kennedy's annual visits to Paris, she and I got into a bit of an argument: I wanted to have a limousine meet her at the plane and she said she would just take a cab. I thought it was a foolish economy for a woman her age after such a long trip and said so. Eunice, who had overheard my protestations, later said to me, "Mother's saving all her money for her relatives, so they can ride around in limousines after she's gone." Occasionally, even Mrs. Kennedy began to feel that she might have been too generous. In a letter to one of her Fitzgerald nephews, she commented astringently, "The Kennedy family money is not limitless."

She may have felt compelled to make that observation because the relatives were never reluctant to ask her for money. At the first sign of difficulty, they would turn to Aunt Rose, and although she might initially be irritated by the request, she would usually say yes. One niece, who had for a time been on welfare, received a subsidy of $10,000 to $15,000 a year from Mrs. Kennedy (she asked me dubiously if that was enough to live on). A nephew who had gotten into some sort of a bind asked Mrs. Kennedy to tide him over the rough spot, and she arranged to have the New York office send him $400 a month as a temporary measure. Then she forgot all about the matter. Several years later, the New York office asked me if I could discreetly find out if this fellow still needed the money. I tried to discuss it with Mrs. Kennedy, but I could see she didn't remember anything about it. Since no one wanted to push Mrs. Kennedy on the subject, the stipend continued—and for all I know is still being paid to this very day.

In addition to the outright gifts of money, Mrs. Kennedy

helped in other ways. She lent her sisters-in-law her fur coats or her designer hats for special occasions. All the nieces and nephews were invited either to Palm Beach or Hyannis Port for an annual vacation. In Hyannis Port, they were generally given the unused apartment over the garage, formerly the chauffeur's quarters. But she always saw to it that the refrigerator was stocked with milk, orange juice, eggs, bread, sodas, butter, and a cold roast chicken. I once commented to Mrs. Kennedy that I thought it was nice of her to do that for her relatives every year, and she answered, "That's all right, my dear. My relatives are all nice people and none of them have any money. This is just a little something I can do for them." I gathered that not all of them were completely grateful. One year, a nephew asked Mrs. Kennedy if she could send him money so he could take a "real" vacation in Kennebunkport, Maine, instead of going to Hyannis Port. She was hurt by the request, but eventually she did give him the money he asked for.

There was a catch to her generosity, though. Those who accepted it were perennially treated like poor relatives by the Kennedy side of the family. It was very noticeable that Mrs. Kennedy's own children never mixed with "the relatives." Usually the relatives were only invited when the children weren't planning to be around; and if the children did happen to come at the same time, they barely seemed to recognize the visitors. It was really like a caste system, and "the relatives" were definitely at the bottom of the heap.

I noticed this attitude even in the Kennedys' treatment of Joe Gargan. The son of Rose's sister Agnes, Joe had spent most of his summers with the Kennedys after his mother died in 1936. He was especially close to Teddy, but he seemed devoted to all the family. He lived near them in Hyannis Port and looked after Mrs. Kennedy's house in the winter, going out of his way to keep an eye on the whole compound. Yet Joe was still undeniably "second string." When he brought his family to visit in Palm Beach, Mrs. Kennedy told him one night at dinner that his family ate much more than her children did. She suggested that they cut back on chocolate-chip cookies and added she was instructing the cook to cut pompano from the menu to compensate for the cost of their larger helpings.

I couldn't help but feel sorry for some of these guests, especially the ones who had no idea what they were letting themselves in for. I'll never forget the niece of Mr. Kennedy's who came to visit in Palm Beach. It was her first trip down in more than a decade. Her initial surprise came when I was the one to meet her and her daughter at the airport (in my little Plymouth Duster), rather than a chauffeur with a big car. All the way back to the house, she chatted about the good times she had had when she visited Uncle Joe there. She asked if his cabin cruiser was still there (of course, it was long gone) and continued to reminisce about past glories. I knew the poor woman was in for a shock and tried to prepare her for it.

But not even I realized just how awful their visit was going to be until we got back to the house. Naturally the staff the niece remembered was conspicuously absent. The only person available to help them struggle upstairs with their luggage was yours truly. Then when we went back downstairs to the vast and silent kitchen to look for something cold to drink, we discovered there was absolutely nothing in the refrigerator. Apparently the cook-maid had decided to go on strike when faced with the job of cooking and cleaning for these two extra people; she refused even to do the grocery shopping. So Mrs. Kennedy entertained these bewildered relatives while I rushed out to the store for a few necessities. Later, when the chauffeur got back from his regular nine-to-five job elsewhere, he went to the supermarket to stock up.

By the next day, I had managed to get a temporary cook to come in to prepare a few evening meals that week. The guests had to fix their own breakfasts; for lunch, I drove them into town to a restaurant. Sometimes on my way home in the evening, I would drop them off at a shopping mall or a movie, just to give them the chance to get out of the house for a few hours (of course, they had to take a taxi back). It was obvious that they still weren't getting enough to eat, since I kept finding candy wrappers in their room. The poor niece never got over her initial shock, and for an entire week she wore a stunned expression on her face. She wrote a very nice thank-you letter afterward, but needless to say, she never came back.

Yet many of the relatives did come back year after year. Whatever the discomforts, they still wanted to see Mrs. Kennedy and counted themselves lucky to be part of the magic. And Mrs. Kennedy, too, never ceased to value the members of her extended family, the clan she delighted in serving as matriarch.

5

Palm Beach

The place to observe all of the members of the extended Kennedy family, at their best and their worst, was Palm Beach. Mrs. Kennedy usually arrived at her home there in time for Thanksgiving, and she left shortly after Easter. In the interim, streams of visiting children, grandchildren, in-laws, and other relatives poured across the threshold. But for the life of me, I could never figure out why all those people wanted to go there.

My own first look inside the Palm Beach house was un-utterably depressing. I traveled down from Hyannis Port in early October 1974 on the autotrain that took me and my car to Sanford, Florida, which was several hours' drive from Palm Beach. My first problem was merely finding the place. The Kennedy house is located on North Ocean Boulevard, locally called Millionaires Row because of the cost of the lavish oceanfront houses spread along its length. But as is frequently the case in wealthy neighborhoods, few street addresses were visible on mailboxes or front gates; the residents don't want to be found by the casually curious. After driving back and forth a few times, I finally stopped a gardener working on someone's elegantly manicured lawn and asked if he knew where the Kennedys lived. He pointed down the road to a curve that was bordered by the rare sight of un-developed land. "Just look for the dark red doors," he said.

At first glimpse, the house seemed like a fortress. A tall hedge ran the length of the property on North Ocean Boulevard, punctuated by only a few openings; a big door painted dark red, with iron straps and huge circular handles, that presumably led to the front door; a pair of garage doors; and a little arched doorway in the hedge. I could see the Spanish-style house, with its white stucco exterior and red tile roof, but I couldn't find a way to get into it. Just as I was about to give up and go look for a phone, I noticed a driveway at the north side of the estate that led to a paved parking lot (I later learned that Joe Kennedy had put this in during his son's presidency). There the white stucco wall was pierced by a wooden gate, which turned out to be unlocked. A short walk led me to a flight of stone steps that climbed to the kitchen door. It too was unlocked. I called out "Hello" but got no answer, so I boldly entered.

I was in a high-ceilinged room that seemed to be an adjunct to the kitchen. It contained three large freezers of the type you might find in a restaurant or hotel and a big metal table. Next to it was the kitchen proper. It had two stoves and a refrigerator, with cabinets built in all around. Everything in sight was dirty and shabby, and at least a generation out-of-date. I couldn't imagine anyone actually turning out meals in such a place. Walking on toward what I hoped was the center of the house, I entered the butler's pantry, where glass-fronted cupboards held an array of dishes and glassware. This room alone was bigger than most people's kitchens. The three rooms together were obviously de-signed for the staging of large banquets for many guests.

Before I could penetrate any further, I was greeted effu-sively by an attractive and vivacious elderly woman with snow-white hair. She gave me a big hug of welcome and then intro-duced herself as "Mam'selle." I later learned that Mam'selle had been with the Kennedy family for many years. Back in the 1950s and '60s, she was governess to the four Lawford children; after Pat and Peter were divorced and the youngest child was school age, she was let go. A few years later, she began to work for

Mrs. Kennedy during the winters in Palm Beach. Currently she acted as a combination cook and maid, the same job Jeannette had in the summers in Hyannis Port. Mam'selle was of course French, and despite the fact that she had been in this country for decades, she still retained a thick French accent. When she pronounced my name, it came out "Babella."

Mam'selle whisked me through the house on a quick tour. To my surprise, the dominant effect was of shabbiness—makeshift decor imposed over the fading grandeur of the original building. The house had been designed by famed Florida architect Addison Mizner, back in the mid-1920s, for one of the wealthy Philadelphia Wanamakers. The skeleton of the house was beautiful and clearly designed for lavish living. The most unusual feature was a long passageway, roofed but not enclosed, that led from the door of the hedge past a charming garden area over a stone patio and up to the front door. It was an architectural idea borrowed from a cloister and it conveyed a lovely sense of green peace.

Opening off the entry foyer were an immense dining room to the left and living room to the right, both with windows overlooking the ocean and the front lawn dotted with palms. The floors of those rooms were laid in attractive rosy Cuban tile; the architectural detail was executed in grainy, long-lasting pecky cypress; and the walls of the foyer were rough lava stone, with that lovely but treacherous stone staircase rising in a curve. The house had six large bedrooms facing the sea and four smaller ones for live-in domestics which looked out over the vacant lot to the north, which Joe Kennedy had bought to prevent others from building there. The house had all the amenities expected by the rich: a tennis court, a swimming pool surrounded by pink and gray stone laid in an irregular pattern, a row of dressing rooms complete with showers for the use of swimmers and tennis players, a private entrance to the beach set into the seawall with more dressing rooms for ocean swimmers, and patios on three sides of the house.

But what struck me most forcibly was how run-down and shabby everything was. The house itself was in bad repair, with red tiles falling off the roof and wooden window frames rotting away. Falling coconuts had cracked the glass-topped tables on the patio. Some sort of rust had attacked the stone around the pool and produced ugly stains like dried blood on the elegant pattern. Everything in sight cried out for a good coat of paint. The interior was in even worse shape. Some of the curtains in the bedrooms were so damaged by years of exposure to sunlight that they were hanging in shreds. The old linoleum floors in the kitchen, covered with years of greasy dirt, buckled and crumbled. Upholstered furniture was stained and torn.

Efforts to improve matters had only made them worse. Someone who had painted the walls had simply covered everything in sight: hinges, window pulls, electrical outlets, and even brass locks on the doors. To my horror, this painting was carried to its most extreme point of insensitivity in the dining room. The heavy dark wooden furniture, designed by Addison Mizner in a Spanish colonial style to suit the decor, had been painted white with a flat wall paint, and of course it was already showing the dirt. As I walked from one dingy room to another, it was simply impossible to believe that this was the home of one of the richest families in the United States.

Most depressing of all, from a personal point of view, was the room that would be my office. I nearly burst into tears when I saw it. Situated in what had once been a maid's bedroom, at the opposite end of the back hall from Mrs. Kennedy's room, it still had a rusty old sink in one corner of the room. The window was shaded with a tattered venetian blind, and the room was furnished with a white washstand and a white chest of drawers apparently left over from its previous incarnation as a maid's room. Untrimmed bougainvillea was actually growing inside the walls. The only office furniture was a rusty typewriter table that must have been at least thirty years old, and the pleasant surprise of a lovely dark wood secretary that held some books and a few office supplies. There was no desk at all; a small three-drawer metal file cabinet was hidden away in the closet. Dominating the entire room was a truly hideous overstuffed chair, larger than any other piece of furniture in sight. I couldn't bear the thought of spending hours every day in such dreary surroundings.

Eventually I was able to make that office almost bearable. With the approval of the New York office, I brought a desk and put up some curtains. I even got the hideous chair moved to another room. But all that would happen later. My office turned out to be the least of my immediate worries.

The next morning, after an uneasy sleep that was constantly interrupted by the pounding of the surf, which made the whole house shudder, I began to make a list of the things that should be done before Mrs. Kennedy came back from her annual fall shopping trip to Paris. The tennis court was covered with palm leaves and dead branches, weeds were growing up through its surface, and the net was dangling askew. The pool was empty except for about three inches of water in the bottom, and it looked as if someone had started to paint it and abandoned the job months ago. The grass hadn't been cut for weeks, and the hedges and shrubs all needed trimming. Of course, the house itself required a thorough heavy cleaning. Also, since the previous chauffeur had been fired in the spring, a new one had to be hired. And I quickly discovered that the chauffeur's quarters needed a lot of work just to make them habitable. Not only was the kitchen covered with grime and piled high with dirty dishes, the curtains and bed linens were gone and the mattresses were lumpy and stained: The two bedrooms looked like the inside of a cheap motel. To top it all off, there was a huge swarm of bees buzzing around the bare light bulb in the bathroom, all very active and quite annoyed at the thought of sharing their territory with a human being.

I tried to find out how things had gotten into such a mess. Both Mam'selle and Jim, the Palm Beach policeman who worked nights and weekends for Mrs. Kennedy as a combination security guard and caretaker, made it clear that they had been given no responsibility for making decisions about what needed to be done and who should do it. The gardener worked for a landscaping service that maintained the grounds, so he came only when the service sent him. There was no chauffeur or handyman. No one was in charge . . . with predictable results.

At my wit's end, I called Tom Walsh at the New York office and explained the situation to him. "There's so much to do in this big house," I said in panic, "and so little time to do it in, if we're going to be ready when Mrs. Kennedy arrives."

"That's all right, sweetheart," answered Tom, who was always a tower of strength. "You just do whatever you think is necessary and send me the bills." I thanked him and went right to work. I asked the landscaping service to come in and clean up the yard and clear away the branches and leaves from the tennis court, pool, and patios. A cleaning service sent a team of burly men to do the heavy work of polishing the tile floors, washing all the windows inside and out, scouring the bathrooms, and scrubbing the kitchen floors. When they finished with the house, they even managed to make the garage apartment livable, and the county agricultural agent sent someone around to collect the bees. Meanwhile, professionals were sandblasting and repainting the pool. Since Mrs. Kennedy's daily swim was an important element of her routine, I wanted the pool to be ready and waiting for her. Each of the bills for these services was hundreds of dollars, but there was simply no other way. I approved them all and sent them to New York—to be paid out of Mrs. Kennedy's account. I felt a little nervous about this; I had only worked for Mrs. Kennedy a few months and suddenly I was entrusted with decisions involving what seemed to me to be large sums of money. But, at least, when Mrs. Kennedy finally arrived, the house was ready for her. And I was ready for a long rest!

I really never did understand why the Palm Beach house was always so shabby. For investment reasons alone, it was silly to let a piece of prime real estate lose its value. And surely it would have been worth spending a little bit of the Kennedy fortune to make the house where Mrs. Kennedy spent half of the year attractive, or at least comfortable. In answer to my tactful (I hope) questions about the situation, Mrs. Kennedy told me the problem was that the house wasn't hers. Joe Kennedy's will left it to the children, with the stipulation that his widow was to remain in it for her lifetime. Mrs. Kennedy thus felt it wasn't her place to go ahead with repairs and renovations. I suppose the children, for their part, were reluctant to act like impatient landlords and begin making improvements right under their mother's feet, even when they could see the need for them. The result of this impasse was that the house simply went a little further downhill every year. Mrs. Kennedy once commented that maintaining a house on the ocean was like keeping up a ship . . . and I thought this ship was in danger of sinking.

But the shabbiness of the house never stopped people from wanting to visit. From Thanksgiving on, the hordes descended. They never came in just twos or threes, it seemed, but in big groups, all at once. Either Mrs. Kennedy was alone or she was swamped with company. During holidays, especially Thanksgiving, New Year's, and Easter, the house would be jammed, with every bed taken—and sometimes also a few cots rented to take care of the overflow. Just watching all the commotion was enough to make me feel tired at the end of the day.

Perhaps that was why Mrs. Kennedy always clung to her accustomed routine, no matter how many visitors she might have. Her own day started around eight o'clock, when she got up and dressed for church. She usually wore a simple cotton dress, perhaps one of the pretty floral prints she bought at Lilly Pulitzer on Worth Avenue; generally she also put on a hat. Dennis, the chauffeur, drove her in to St. Edward's Church, just a few miles south on the road to the center of town. Although the front entrance of the church (built in the 1920s) is beautifully designed in the Baroque style, with elaborate twisted columns flanking each of the three arched doors, Mrs. Kennedy usually preferred to enter through the simple side door and slip into her customary pew, near the front on the left-hand side. As a regular parishioner, Mrs. Kennedy made an annual gift to the church, usually about five hundred dollars. Some years earlier, she and her husband had also donated one of the lovely stained-glass windows lining the nave. Every morning she put one dollar in the collection box, never more and never less. She would have me cash a check every month and get crisp new singles for this purpose.

When mass was over, she left by the side door and met Dennis, who escorted her across the street to the parking lot (he also attended mass). Dennis was the very same chauffeur who had been let go the previous spring. The only replacement I had been able to find was so young and inexperienced that Mrs. Kennedy was not comfortable with him. So Dennis returned, and things went on as they had before. The main drawback to Dennis was that he had a regular nine-to-five job as a lifeguard at the Sailfish Club, just up the road from the Kennedy house, so he was unavailable during the day. When he did reappear at the end of the day, he was deaf to any requests that he help out by taking out the trash or doing a bit of cleaning. But he was willing to live in the apartment over the garage, and so there was a man on the premises at night. And where Mrs. Kennedy was concerned, he was always willing to do as he was told.

Usually Dennis drove Mrs. Kennedy right back home after mass, stopping only to pick up her morning newspapers. But sometimes she would have errands to do or a function to attend. On those mornings, I would pick her up in the parking lot and do the driving for her, leaving Dennis free to hurry off to his other job. Invariably, when I arrived at the parking lot, the same spectacle met my eyes: Mrs. Kennedy eating her breakfast. She never ate before she left home because she wanted to take communion, so if she planned to go on to other places, she would take her breakfast with her—a thermos of coffee and some slices of toast. The funny part is that she wouldn't eat this breakfast inside her car, because she was afraid she might spill something on the seat. So she stood up in the parking lot, with the cars whizzing by. Dennis handed her a cup for a sip of coffee, took it back and handed her a slice of toast for a bite, took it back and handed her a napkin, then started all over again with the cup of coffee.

But most days, she breakfasted at home. When she got back to the house, she walked in the kitchen door and went directly to the dining room, where she ate alone, sitting at the head of the twenty-foot table surrounded by twelve chairs. The meal consisted of French bread (the only kind of bread that didn't upset her stomach), sliced one inch thick and lightly toasted, served with a little butter and honey. To wash it down, she drank Sanka, in which she dissolved a package of gelatin to make her fingernails strong and her hair glossy. It was her habit to dunk the bread in the coffee, and the general messiness made many guests reluctant to breakfast with her. On very special occasions, she might ask Mam'selle to fix her an egg, too, but normally there was no change from the routine. It seemed like such a shame . . . she had someone in the kitchen who would make anything she asked for. Yet she settled for the same meal every morning of her life.

After breakfast, Mrs. Kennedy took her papers and went upstairs to her room to finish scanning them. She read the *New York Times*, the *Palm Beach Post*, and the *Palm Beach Daily News*, locally known by the nickname of "the shiny sheet" because of the good quality of the paper on which it was printed —it wouldn't do for the society ladies to get ink all over their fingers as they searched the paper for their photographs. She might clip articles of interest about members of the family or people she had met.

When she finished with the papers, Mrs. Kennedy buzzed me (using the intercom button on the telephone) and I walked down the upstairs back hall from my office to her bedroom. The big windows overlooked the bright blue ocean; just sitting on her bed, she had a fabulous view. But I always found the room depressing. The pink-flowered curtains were falling apart at the folds, and their deterioration was hastened by Mrs. Kennedy's attempts to pin them together to prevent the afternoon sunlight from coming in during her naps. The dust ruffle of her bed and the skirt of her vanity were of the same fabric and in little better condition. There was a comfortable chaise, where she usually sat to read, but its faded pink upholstery was dingy and bore ineradicable stains. A bathroom with old-fashioned fixtures stained with rust opened off the bedroom, and there was a roomy walk-in closet, with a safe at the very back for her valuable jewelry.

Usually we went next door to work, in what was called "the

massage room" but was probably originally intended as a dressing room for this master bedroom. Here she had installed a
massage bed, and a masseuse came in once a week. We used
the high bed like a desk top. I sat on one side, in a straight-
backed chair, clutching my steno pad, ready to make notes or
take dictation. She sat on the other side of the bed and fired
away. She would make lists of errands she wanted done, such
as ordering a lamp from Burdines or putting flowers in a guest
room. She dictated letters declining invitations to dinners and
balls, and letters to her children and grandchildren and old
friends. Very personal letters she wrote herself, but most of her
correspondence I typed on her gray stationery with the simple
engraved head that said, "Palm Beach, Florida." More important
letters were typed on the ivory stationery with a blue border.

In addition to taking care of her correspondence, Mrs. Kennedy might give me items to enter in one of her three black
notebooks. The household book was full of miscellaneous house-
wifely tips, such as how to clean lampshades or polish stainless
steel. It was also used for recording addresses of shops and
telephone numbers of workmen. This notebook even contained
such information as Rosemary's shoe size and the address of the
place from which her special shoes could be ordered. The second
notebook was full of Mrs. Kennedy's favorite sayings and quotes,
and she added new entries from her reading of newspapers and
an occasional book. The idea was that she could look it over
before she went to a dinner party and thus be sure of having
something interesting to say. The third notebook was for her
French expressions and was part of her lifelong study of that
language.

By the time we finished going over all these things, it was
time for Mrs. Kennedy's daily swim. Unless I was terribly busy
or she had lots of company, I usually joined her. If the water
was warm and calm, we would go in the sea. Mrs. Kennedy all
dressed to go in the water was a sight to behold. She wore not
one but two bathing caps. One covered the front of her head
and another the back, because, she explained, "I have such a
tremendous head." On top of the caps she wore a sun visor to

shield her sensitive eyes from the strong outdoor light, and she wore sunglasses as well, to double her protection. Over it all went a big straw hat, which she tied to her head with a chiffon scarf. This getup left her unprepared for sudden emergencies. One day, as we were floating peacefully, a big wave came out of nowhere and simply swallowed her up. I dove under the water, put my arms under hers, and pushed her back up to the surface. The sunglasses stayed under, and the straw hat began to float away, with the pink scarf drifting behind it like a tail. Meanwhile, Mrs. Kennedy was gasping from the sudden shock, and her false teeth came loose. It took quite a while to retrieve everything and get her back up on the beach. She was shaken, but it didn't take long for her to recover her usual aplomb. "Too bad," she joked, "there was no one sitting on the beach to take a picture. It would have been in all the papers that you saved my life."

Most of the time we used the pool, which was heated to the eighty-six degrees that her doctor recommended. The machinery for heating the pool was the bane of my existence. Apparently it had been installed back in the 1960s, after Joe Kennedy had his stroke, and the combination of age and the effects of the salt air made it break down with irritating regularity. The actual heating unit was located a few yards away from the pool, in a sort of pit sunk into the yard. During my first winter in Palm Beach, I swear I must have spent a third of my time crouched down in that pit with a succession of repairmen, trying to get the pool heated properly. After weeks of consultation, the man from the pool maintenance service explained that most of the problems came from the fact that the thermostat was constantly being adjusted. When Mrs. Kennedy got into the pool, she would check the temperature of the water coming into the pool. If it wasn't warm enough, she would ask me to turn up the thermostat immediately.

The repairmen explained that the temperature of the water coming into the pool would vary—sometimes hot and sometimes cold—producing a mix in the pool of eighty-six degrees. But Mrs. Kennedy never accepted this explanation and continued to ask me to move the thermostat up or down, according to the temperature of the water coming into the pool at the moment. I finally developed a technique of bending over and making a big show of adjusting the control without ever actually touching it. Yet still the mechanism malfunctioned frequently.

I concluded that perhaps someone else was playing with the thermostat when I wasn't around. So I had the repairmen install a padlock on the door of the control box, and I kept the key myself. When Mrs. Kennedy and I went swimming, I would take the key and open the door to pretend to make the adjustments she asked for. The rest of the time, the door would be locked and no one else could tamper with the temperamental machinery. Yet we continued to have trouble, and I kept noticing that the thermostat had been changed, and once I even saw on the ground nearby a big stick that had been used to pry open the padlocked door. Mam'selle, Dennis, and Jim all denied doing any such thing. Eventually it dawned on me that our culprit was none other than Mrs. Kennedy herself! She was still determined to make that thing work the way she thought it ought to.

The battle of the thermostat continued for weeks, until the day that she put her hand in front of the place where the water flowed in and it suddenly sucked her arm in the hole, right up to the shoulder. She of course screamed and thrashed around in the pool, so I hurriedly swam to her aid. Mrs. Kennedy seemed to be caught in some powerful suction, and tugging on her arm didn't help. I finally hit on the idea of rotating her arm, and that broke the pressure and she was released at last. I helped her down to the shallow end of the pool and she stood there trembling. Spontaneously I reached out for her hand and held it up to the warmth of my face, in the kind of gesture you might use to comfort a child, and she began to calm down. Once she got over her fright, she snatched her hand away quickly, as if to demonstrate that she was perfectly all right and didn't need any help from anyone. Although I knew she appreciated my aid, she was as determined as ever about her independence.

That incident put an end to her attempts to gauge the warmth of the incoming water, but unfortunately the pool heating system got worse and worse. The maintenance people told me that the only cure was to install a new filter, which would permit the warm water to flow into the pool at a faster rate. When Mrs. Kennedy heard it would cost more than four hundred dollars, she refused to agree, saying she would just give up her swim on cold days.

But I knew how much her daily swim meant to her. It was good for her physical health and perhaps even more important for her mental health. I think she went to the pool to work out her emotions, to fight her way back to her usual calm. I remember one time when she was obviously very distressed by some news about Rosemary, who had started to have convulsions when her medication was changed. We went in swimming that morning, but instead of her usual chatter, Mrs. Kennedy said simply, "I don't want to talk now. I have something I need to think about." Then she paddled furiously back and forth across the pool until she nearly reached the point of exhaustion. Recently I read a book in which the writer mentioned that Rose Kennedy went in swimming as usual on the day of her husband's death and cited the fact as evidence of her coldness toward him. But anyone who knew Mrs. Kennedy would realize that sticking to her daily routine of a swim was simply her way of coping with any overwhelming emotion.

On the increasingly frequent days when the pool heating system wasn't working right, Mrs. Kennedy would ask me to drive her down to Mary Sanford's house for a swim. Mary, a former starlet who had married wealthy Stephen ("Laddie") Sanford, was one of Mrs. Kennedy's few real friends in Palm Beach. According to the rumors of decades past, Joe Kennedy had been strongly attracted to Mary; if that was true, Mrs. Kennedy's friendship is just another example of her aristocratic ability to ignore the obvious when it was disagreeable. By the mid-1970s, Laddie Sanford had been bedridden for years after a stroke, and Mary, although getting on in years herself, still ruled as the acknowledged leader of Palm Beach society.

I always loved to go there, because the Sanford home was like something out of a 1930s movie. We swam in the indoor pool, small and deep, with a soothing whirlpool. (There was a big outdoor heated pool as well.) Statues lined the pool, and there were complete dressing rooms nearby. One wall was covered with a mural of a mermaid diving down to a large pile of jewelry, and that part of the mural was actually underwater. Mrs. Kennedy told me that the bare-breasted mermaid in the mural was supposed to be Mary, adding that she thought it was "rather obscene." In front of the diving mermaid, there was a casual living room with comfortably upholstered furniture and a glass-topped dining room table where meals could be served. To me, it symbolized the luxurious life I'd always imagined to be the rule in Palm Beach.

Mary Sanford was always hospitable, but swimming there was not a long-term solution to the pool problem. After some discussion with the pool service people, I came up with a scheme to replace the filter without letting Mrs. Kennedy know—another one of those "Don't tell Mrs. Kennedy" episodes. With the blessing of the New York office, I arranged to replace the filter by breaking the job up into little steps that could be done each afternoon while Mrs. Kennedy had her nap. The most difficult aspect of this scheme was that the only way to reach the pool from the parking lot where the workmen left their truck was around the ocean front of the house and thus directly below Mrs. Kennedy's bedroom windows. I held my breath as the workmen carried the new, heavy metal parts in and the old ones out; with that sixth sense that told her when people were trying to put something over on her, Mrs. Kennedy would surely wake up and catch us in the act. But luck was with us, and the repairs were completed in secret. After that, the heating system worked well, and our daily swim became much more enjoyable.

After her swim, Mrs. Kennedy would go back upstairs to her bedroom to change for lunch. Her usual outfit was a pair of pajamas (usually pink with a bit of lace around the Peter Pan collar), a belted robe (also in pink or a pink-and-white print) and pale pink Daniel Green slippers with a hard sole. That's the way she would appear in the dining room, promptly at one o'clock, unless she was expecting a special guest. Her lunch was cooked and served by Mam'selle, and it was always a hot meal. She would have a chop or some chicken, rice or more French bread, possibly a pureed vegetable such as carrots, made tasty with the addition of butter and cream. One of her favorite desserts was a gelatin made with fresh Florida orange juice and covered with cream—and, of course, a sugar cookie or two to go with it.

While Mrs. Kennedy was eating, often totally alone in that large dining room, I had my own lunch. I quickly discovered that going into town on my lunch hour was impossible. By the time I drove there and back, I had only about ten minutes left to gulp down a sandwich. But I could never find anything in Mrs. Kennedy's refrigerator that I might use to get my own meal at the house. Luckily Mam'selle solved my problem by offering to fix my lunch when she prepared her own. So she and I fell into the custom of eating our own lunch in the maids' dining room while Mrs. Kennedy ate hers alone in the main dining room. (Mam'selle would have to jump up once or twice to serve Mrs. Kennedy's next course.)

Mam'selle was actually a wonderful cook, although she tried to conceal it from Mrs. Kennedy so she wouldn't take advantage of the fact and expect her to cook for guests. She prepared quite elegant little lunches, and I began often to pick up an accompanying bottle of wine on my way to work. It would have been sheer bliss except for the surroundings. If most of the Kennedy house in Palm Beach was shabby, you can imagine what the rooms guests never saw were like. The maids' dining room had a Formica table, like you would find in a cheap coffee shop, with four kitchen chairs in various states of disrepair. There was a lumpy old daybed covered with a dingy bedspread and an elderly rocker whose stuffing threatened to emerge at any moment.

There was one redeeming feature of the maids' dining room, though. It contained a huge closet known as the "telephone room," which was the control center of the complex phone system Joe Kennedy had installed decades earlier. It enabled calls to be taken anywhere, but once connected, that phone could not be overheard from any other extension. The telephone room proved to be a wonderful hiding place.

What, you may wonder, did we have to hide? For one thing, our lunch. Although Mrs. Kennedy wanted the staff to eat in, we were always uncomfortable (like generations of "downstairs staff" before us) when she actually saw us eating. Whenever we heard her footsteps heading for our little sanctuary, Mam'selle and I quickly shoved our plates in the telephone room and concealed all traces of our luncheon menu. Mrs. Kennedy found us quietly reading the morning paper or watching a game show on television. The same hiding place was used by Mam'selle on her day off when she would leave me a lovely little cold plate for my lunch.

Occasionally, the telephone room was even used to conceal people. For example, Jim, the security guard, sometimes dropped in to chat, a habit Mrs. Kennedy opposed because she expected him to be out guarding the property. So at the sound of her footsteps, Jim would duck into the telephone room and remain there until Mrs. Kennedy left. He did the same thing in my office upstairs, using the clothes closet there, and sometimes relatives or grandchildren also ducked into these hiding places. It was often simpler to disappear than to explain to Mrs. Kennedy what you were up to.

After Mrs. Kennedy finished her lunch, she went upstairs to take a nap, actually getting into bed and closing all the curtains. That was the time I could count on to get my own work done: writing letters and making phone calls to take care of the things we had discussed that morning. But the calm lasted only a few hours. Mrs. Kennedy would be up again by three or three-thirty. If the weather was particularly nice, she might take another swim. Frequently she decided to go shopping on Worth Avenue or to make an appointment at the Elizabeth Arden salon to get her hair done. Since I had to drive her wherever she was going, I often accompanied her on these errands. Mrs. Kennedy loved to shop at Saks Fifth Avenue, the Courrèges boutique, and Kassatly's, a Palm Beach store renowned for its beautiful household linens. The clerks all along Worth Avenue were familiar with her . . . and her sudden changes of mind. She would, for example, select a skirt and even go so far as to have it pinned up for alterations and then decide at the last minute not to take it. Or, more commonly, she would buy a dress one day and return it the next (and then perhaps do the same thing all over again the following week with the same dress). One day, when we were returning a dress at Saks, one of the clerks said to me, "It's getting to the point where these dresses that Mrs. Kennedy buys are just taking a ride, aren't they?" She added tolerantly, "Oh, well, I guess we'll just chalk it up to public relations." The magic of the Kennedy name remained powerful.

The hairdressers at Elizabeth Arden were equally used to Mrs. Kennedy's foibles. She liked to have her hair done every week in Palm Beach, but she didn't have the patience to sit idly under the dryer for very long. She would insist that they take the rollers out while the back of her hair was still wet, and then she complained about the way it looked. Finally the hairdressers worked out a system of sending her home with the rollers still in place, and then she combed it out herself.

Whatever our errands, we were usually back at the house a little before five. Then Mrs. Kennedy changed into slacks and a pullover and her funny-looking shoes to go out for her daily walk. It was just two short blocks across to the paved sidewalk that runs along the shore of Lake Worth, in front of the big houses there. She walked for about an hour, sometimes stopping at one of the benches along the way for a brief rest before she continued. If the children or grandchildren were visiting, one of them would go along with her. It was the ideal time for a quiet and private talk.

Mrs. Kennedy liked to get home to watch the six o'clock news on television in the comfortable little den right off the dining room. It was paneled in warm wood, had built-in book-cases and a door that opened onto the patio. The walls were hung with memorabilia, most notably Jack's handwritten draft of his inaugural address. Houseguests might join her there, or there might be a cocktail hour in the living room instead. Teddy might fix his daiquiris for the crowd, or Pat Lawford would make her favorite bullshots. Then dinner was served promptly at seven. It was another hot meal, almost identical to her lunch, although if she had company, she might plan a more elaborate menu for them. Roast beef was always popular, along with the creamed vegetables Mrs. Kennedy favored. Dessert might be Baskin-Robbins English toffee ice cream topped with butterscotch sauce.

After dinner, Mrs. Kennedy generally retired to her room, where Mam'selle had left a little tray containing a thermos of hot milk and some slices of toasted French bread in case she felt hungry before she went to sleep. She might read for a while. She liked biographies and books about current events, especially when she had met the leading characters. Fiction she read only rarely, and she didn't care for the contemporary style of sexual frankness. I remember one time she asked me to get her a copy of *Jaws* when she heard the grandchildren talking about it. Apparently she read only as far as the first sex scene, for the next morning she returned the book to me with the terse comment "Burn this, it's trash." Since her eyesight was failing, she couldn't read anything for very long, so she often watched television instead. She liked documentaries and news specials and avoided the shows meant for entertainment only. Her children and grandchildren were very good about calling her in the evenings, just to say hello and bring her up to date on family news, and that helped her pass the time.

Mrs. Kennedy was generally in bed by eleven. Sometimes she remained wakeful and prowled around the house in the wee hours of the night. The next morning, Mam'selle would complain that she hadn't been able to sleep because Mrs. Kennedy had taken a bath at 1:00 A.M. Or I might find illegible notes scribbled on my steno pad, things she had thought of while unable to sleep.

I used to reflect on the difference between Mrs. Kennedy's life-style and that of her neighbors in Palm Beach. She had more money than most of them, more friends in high places, more powerful contacts. She had a closetful of beautiful ball gowns that she had bought in Paris, and even though she had sold some of her jewelry, she still had some fabulous pieces, such as a triple-strand pearl necklace with a diamond clasp, a ten-carat diamond ring, and some elaborate diamond drop earrings. Mrs. Kennedy could have been the queen of Palm Beach society. Yet she rarely went out at all. She attended one or two of the big charity balls of the season—the Heart Ball and the Cancer Ball—and that was about the extent of her social life. She didn't lunch or shop with friends. She didn't dine out at other people's houses, and she rarely invited anyone to hers. "The house is too shabby to entertain" was her excuse. She didn't attend the openings and previews where women wore their designer originals and were photographed for the shiny sheet. When she bought tickets for some benefit, she often gave them away. Several times Mrs. Kennedy offered me tickets for some glamorous event, such as an appearance by Bob Hope at the Royal Poinciana Theater for the benefit of cancer research; she was willing to contribute the money to a good cause but she didn't want to go to the event. Her existence was solitary, removed from the social whirl that was going on all around her, barely touched by the status competition that is so much a part of Palm Beach life.

Of course, she wasn't always literally alone, because in Palm Beach, the family was likely to descend at any moment. Yet even when the house was full of guests, Mrs. Kennedy remained aloof. When the relatives or the grandchildren came to visit, she always greeted them on their arrival, but then she would retire to the security of her usual routine, seeing the visitors only at mealtimes. Thus she tried to remain unbothered by the constant turmoil going on in the house. That, I discovered, was my responsibility.

The first problem was finding the domestic staff to cope with the needs of our visitors. Mam'selle refused to cook for company, so a cook had to be found whenever we had more than one or two guests. Some guests brought their own domestics with them to help out. When the Morton Downeys came to dinner, bringing Gary Cooper's widow and her husband, Dr. John Converse, they also brought their own maid to serve the meal. Jean Smith often brought her maid, and both Eunice and Pat occasionally came with a cook. But, of course, it was hard for them to function efficiently in a strange kitchen, and the quality of the meals was often disappointing.

One solution was to try to get a cook from one of the domestic employment services in Palm Beach. Unfortunately, the services knew all about the Kennedys: the low wages, the long hours and hard work in that badly equipped kitchen, the sudden dismissal when the visitors left. So it was all I could do to talk them into sending anyone at all, let alone the cream of the crop. A few good cooks passed through our kitchen, but they were usually available just for a week or so while their regular employers were out of town. Others were either incompetent or nutty—and even those were often unwilling to stay. One of them quit after she tried to get back into the house on her afternoon off. No one heard her shout and knock on the gate, and as I had discovered on my own initial arrival, there was no way in if the door in the side gate wasn't left open. So the poor woman walked down to the beach and then somehow managed to climb up the twelve-foot seawall to get onto the grounds. Mrs. Kennedy and I laughed at this exploit, but the cook was not amused.

The best solution to our staff problem was to hire temporarily a woman who had formerly cooked for the Senator in Washington and was now living in Palm Beach. Nellie was a good soul and an even better cook. Her credentials included stints with Millicent Hearst, Cary Grant, and Gloria Vanderbilt. Of course, she knew how to make all the Kennedy family favorites: the sugar cookies for Mrs. Kennedy, the chocolate roll for the Senator, and her famous chocolate-chip cookies that everybody loved. Nellie was in semiretirement but was willing to come back and work for Mrs. Kennedy during part of the winter. The only problem was Mrs. Kennedy herself: she simply didn't understand the kind of pay appropriate to a good cook in that day and age. Finally, in collusion with the New York office, I came up with a solution. ("Don't tell Mrs. Kennedy," I warned Nellie.) Mrs. Kennedy paid Nellie the thirty-five dollars a day she thought was the top salary any cook could expect, and the New York office paid her the extra fifteen dollars a day that brought the total up to the lowest figure Nellie was willing to consider. So when the house was full of people, Nellie would cook and Mam'selle would clean and sometimes help with the serving of the meals. It was still too small a staff to do everything for six or ten guests, especially when some of them expected breakfast in bed and other special services. But at least there was good food on the table.

Yet every week, a new crisis with the staff would erupt. Mrs. Kennedy would decide, during a lull when she had no guests, that she didn't really need Nellie and tell her to leave. Or during the peak holiday periods when every bed in the house was full, Nellie herself would threaten to leave because she could not go on working eighteen hours every day. She would agree to stay only if we would hire a second maid to take over some of the chores. So then I would be calling the service again, trying to find someone willing to come in temporarily. Of course, since Mrs. Kennedy was not even fully convinced that we needed Nellie, she was even more reluctant to go to the additional expense of a second maid. When I tried to explain to her that we simply couldn't manage with only the one cook-maid when there were guests in the house, she replied that she would just tell everyone not to come. When I pressed her on the subject, she said stubbornly, "I know how I want to live my life and I know how I want everything done."

I was generally caught right in the middle. My job was to please Mrs. Kennedy, and I knew she was upset by the strange faces and the mounting bills. Yet I also sympathized with Nellie and Mam'selle, who worked long and hard under difficult conditions. Nellie, for example, usually ended up fixing three or four different entrées for the same meal. Mrs. Kennedy would set up the dinner menu and Nellie might therefore prepare roast beef, green beans, a salad, and some sort of dessert. Then in the afternoon Eunice would ask what was planned for dinner and respond dubiously, "I don't really feel like eating roast beef, I'd prefer to have lobster." And Pat would march into the kitchen and give brisk instructions: "Of course, I don't eat red meat, so

I'll just have broiled pompano." The bills for all this food were astronomical. When I sent them to the New York office after one holiday invasion, I got an immediate call from one of the men there. "What are you people eating down there?" he asked. "Gold nuggets?" In fact, it wasn't like a home at all, but more like cooking in a restaurant.

Or maybe an institution. At times the chaos was unbelievable. I had to post lists on the bulletin board in the kitchen to let people know who was arriving when and where they were staying. Here, from my notes, is one such schedule.

SCHEDULE

WEDNESDAY, MARCH 19, 1975

ARRIVING: Mrs. Smith   2:45 P.M.
                Amanda Smith   National #95
                Kym Smith
                William Smith
                Robin Lawford
                Bridie (Smith
                  governess)
                Jean Bowers
                  (Smith maid)
                Mary Connelly
                  (Lawford cook)

FRIDAY, MARCH 21

ARRIVING: Mrs. Lawford   5:12 P.M.
                Victoria Lawford   Eastern #195

ROOM ARRANGEMENT

Mrs. Smith
Amanda Smith   } Lake bedroom

Kym Smith
Bridie   } Ocean bedroom

Robin Lawford Victoria Lawford } Caroline Kennedy	Bedroom next to Mrs. Lawford
William Smith	Bedroom next to Mrs. Kennedy
Jean Bowers	Corner bedroom
Mary Connelly	Rear bedroom on north side

I was making and breaking so many plane reservations in and out of Palm Beach that the ticket agent asked me if I was running a hotel! And since Dennis didn't work between nine and five, I also ended up doing most of the driving back and forth to the airport. The Senator was very good about arranging for his own transportation, but other members of the family expected that to be one of the functions of Mrs. Kennedy's staff. I nearly always drove the grandchildren to and from the airport, and they frequently complained that I drove too slowly. Their parents could be equally demanding. Once I went to meet Pat Lawford and got stuck in the traffic on the bridge from Palm Beach to West Palm Beach, where the airport is located. That made me five minutes late, and when I got there, Pat was nowhere to be seen. Finally I telephoned Mrs. Kennedy and learned Pat had just walked in the door; she had gotten a ride with someone else. The next day I said firmly, "Please don't ask me to go pick up anyone anymore, Mrs. Kennedy." She answered quickly, "I agree."

Easter vacation of 1977 was probably the most frantic time ever. Every bed in the house was taken, and Dennis had even been asked to share his two-bedroom apartment over the garage to hold the overflow. Jean and Pat were there, with most of the Lawford and Smith children. Caroline was there, too (sleeping on a rented cot), and I saw a report in the local paper that Jackie was going to come at the end of the week. We discussed the problem of where she could sleep, and Mrs. Kennedy came up with the notion of putting her on the massage bed. Somehow I couldn't quite visualize the fastidious Jackie tucked away on that high narrow bed in a little room opening off her mother-in-law's. I wasn't too surprised to learn a few days later that Jackie wasn't coming after all.

As usual, we didn't have enough staff to cope with the demands. The second maid I had hired to help out quit. She said working for the Kennedys was making her blood pressure too high and ruining her health. So the next morning, which was Nellie's day off, I came in and found Jean and Pat standing at the big sink in the kitchen, laboriously doing the breakfast dishes. Later that day I saw Caroline on her hands and knees cleaning a rubber mat, with Mrs. Kennedy standing over her to supervise, wearing her usual big hat. And to think these people came here for a vacation!

Meanwhile, with all that crowd of Kennedys in one place, the media were having a field day. There were reporters waiting outside the front gates, patrolling the beach, trying to conceal themselves behind the bushes on a neighbor's property. They were even hovering overhead in a helicopter, hoping to get photos of the granddaughters in their bikinis (they only succeeded in disturbing Jean and Pat as they were playing tennis). They brandished cameras and communicated with one another over walkie-talkies. Most of these journalists were from the *National Enquirer*, and apparently they intended to let nothing stand in the way of getting some sort of scoop. When Mrs. Kennedy went out for her evening walk, they popped up from behind the bushes, whereupon she told them she was just a tourist and it wouldn't be worth taking her picture—but her Boston accent gave her away. Later she asked me to call the Senator's office and see if anything could be done to put a stop to it. An aide reported back, "I talked to our man there and he told me they had gone to considerable expense to get those photographs down there. They won't cancel the operation now."

Although she tried to isolate herself from all the turmoil, Mrs. Kennedy was often badly upset by these periods when so many guests arrived at once. One morning, after a huge Thanksgiving crowd had just left, I found Mrs. Kennedy sitting at the table in the maids' dining room crying uncontrollably. She was distraught because her twelve guests had created such havoc: Lamps had been overturned, towels were left out by the pool and beach, half a turkey disappeared during the night, glasses were broken, possessions left behind that would have to be packed and mailed to the forgetful guest—in other words, the usual aftermath of a Kennedy holiday. I tried to soothe her by assuring her I could get someone in to clean up the mess and set the house back to rights. That calmed her down for a minute, but then she began to cry all over again because she didn't want to hire a strange maid. She just wanted her quiet routine reestablished, with a daily schedule that she felt she could control.

Her distress over these disruptions sometimes led her to cancel visits or ask people not to come. She frequently wrote to her grandchildren to explain that she would be unable to have them visit in Florida or to suggest changing the date of a planned visit to some more convenient time. For example, she wrote Ethel's son David to say that he couldn't come when he wanted to, but added that he might want to reschedule his visit when the Smiths would be there (since they would bring their own staff and the household would thus be more comfortable).

I knew she had really gotten upset when she asked me to call the Senator and tell him not to come down for the weekend as he had planned, since she usually anticipated his visits eagerly. I knew he was not going to like this turn of events, and I dreaded making the call. At first, he merely seemed perplexed: *Why* couldn't he come? I tried to explain how upset she was, how short of staff we were, how difficult it was to look after guests. He listened to all this patiently and then answered, "I'm sure all this is true, but I don't know what to do. I'll speak to my sisters about it." Then he added firmly, "Meanwhile, I would like to come down to Palm Beach." But later he spoke to his mother on the phone and, realizing how distressed she was, canceled his visit.

I was usually very glad to leave that scene of chaos and go home to my own two-bedroom oceanfront apartment in Juno Beach, about a forty-five-minute drive away. Not only was it much more peaceful there, it was also more comfortable. The Kennedy house had neither air conditioning nor central heating. So on those October days when the mercury rose to ninety-five, I sweltered in my small office with inadequate ventilation. And on the not-rare-enough occasions when the temperature dropped into the thirties and forties in the wintertime, everyone in the house had to bundle up against the terrible chill of those stone walls and tile floors. I would go to work wearing heavy tights, lined wool slacks, and two thick sweaters. Poor Mrs. Kennedy felt the cold more than I did. And yet she still went swimming! The air was so cold that steam would come up from the heated pool in billows, and I could only see her head in a bathing cap in the midst of those clouds of steam.

So I would go home at the end of the day, put my feet up, pour myself a glass of wine, and try to relax as I looked out at the ocean. I would think about the funny scene in the kitchen as Nellie stood at the counter making one of her delicious cheese balls, vigorously stirring away and reciting Robert Burns at the top of her voice with her inimitable Scots burr: "Man's inhumanity to man," she quoted, "makes countless thousands mourn." Meanwhile, Mam'selle would run in and out, her French accent dueling with Nellie's Scottish one. Jim Connors, the guard, might stop in for a cup of coffee and add his Southern drawl to the mélange.

"Barrrrrbara," said Nellie.

"Babella," said Mam'selle.

"Bobra," said Jim.

And then . . . "Baaabara," Mrs. Kennedy would call.

Time for another glass of wine.

Then I would think about the Kennedys, and they began to seem like figures out of a comic opera. There was Teddy, standing in the kitchen wearing nothing but a towel wrapped around his waist, while another one of the girlfriends who looked exactly like Joan waited for him in the President's bedroom, the big room on the ground floor with a separate entrance that permitted people to come and go unobserved by Mrs. Kennedy. Or there was Sarge, a formally announced candidate for president who was being protected by the Secret Service, arriving at the house in pomp and circumstance, only to find no one there to greet him. There was one of the relatives who had stayed for a few days, usually out of sight in his room; when I drove him to the airport, he asked me quite casually, "Could we stop off at the hospital? I don't feel well," and ended up being treated in the emergency room for alcohol withdrawal. (He had no money, so I had to pay for it.) Best of all was the sight of Mrs. Kennedy, concerned because I was having trouble pulling the big Lincoln out of our drive onto North Ocean Boulevard due to a hazardous curve, getting out of the backseat of the car, marching out in the middle of the road in her bright pink Courrèges suit and matching pinwheel hat, and holding up her hand to stop the oncoming cars while she motioned me out onto the road. I'll never forget the looks on the faces of the other drivers!

Yes, there were plenty of amusing moments. And yet the memory that lingered the longest was something Mrs. Kennedy said one afternoon as I told her good-bye on my way home at the end of the day. "You're lucky," she said quite seriously. "You can leave when you want to. I'm stuck here."

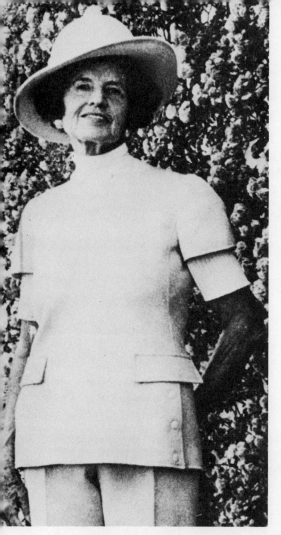

This picture of Rose Kennedy, one of my favorites, was taken the first summer I worked for her as her private secretary. She is wearing an aqua-colored Courrèges pantsuit that she bought in Paris, along with a matching hat, and standing in front of the beautiful roses that flourished in the sea air at the Hyannis Port house. (*AP/Wide World Photos*)

The Hyannis Port house, with Mrs. Kennedy standing in front of it, bundled up for one of her evening walks. The big window upstairs to the right is Mrs. Kennedy's bedroom. (*From the collection of Barbara Gibson*)

The interior of Mrs. Kennedy's bedroom in Hyannis Port. The room is a lovely mixture of floral prints and white eyelet. Her desk (left), was her favorite working and thinking spot. (*From the collection of Barbara Gibson*)

Barbara, at her desk in her cheery Hyannis Port office. (*From the collection of Barbara Gibson*)

Barbara and Jeannette in front of the Hyannis Port house. (*From the collection of Barbara Gibson*)

An aerial view of the Kennedy house in Palm Beach. The parking lot is on the right of the house, the palm shaded pool on the left. The property is protected from the ocean by a 12-foot seawall. (*AP/Wide World Photos*)

This is Mrs. Kennedy on her way to that Washington benefit on behalf of the retarded that she attended as a guest of President and Mrs. Ford. You would never guess by looking at her that she had been sick all week in Palm Beach before she made the trip. Her gown is a Paris original, and her jewelry includes her famous triple strand of pearls. I shopped for two days to find those shoes. (*AP/Wide World Photos*)

The author, Barbara Gibson. (*Photography by Moya*)

More of Mrs. Kennedy's public duties. Here, she is hostess to a gathering of Irish children at the compound with son Ted. (*UPI/Bettmann Newsphoto*)

Mrs. Kennedy attending a campaign party with Ted and his younger son, Patrick (applauding). (*UPI/ Bettmann Newsphotos*)

The cup in Mrs. Kennedy's hand tells you who her favorite candidate is. (*AP/Wide World Photos*)

Mrs. Kennedy making an appearance in Boston on Ted's behalf. That's her nephew Joe Gargan standing behind her. (*AP/ Wide World Photos*)

Mrs. Kennedy and her son, Ted, share a warm moment during a ceremony to dedicate a research institute for the retarded. Mrs. Kennedy's carefully typed speech, and the glasses she needed to read it, are on the table. (*UPI/Bettmann Newsphotos*)

Mrs. Kennedy accompanies the Senator and French President Valery Giscard d'Estaing to lay a wreath at John Kennedy's grave in Arlington, Virginia. (*AP/Wide World Photos*)

Here, a happier occasion—Caroline's graduation from prep school in Concord, Massachusetts. From left to right: John Kennedy, Jacqueline Kennedy Onassis, Caroline Kennedy, Rose Kennedy, Ted Kennedy, and Jackie's mother, Janet Auchincloss. (*UPI/ Bettmann Newsphotos*)

Mrs. Kennedy and her grandsons, Christopher Kennedy (left) and Patrick Kennedy (right), share a laugh. (*AP/Wide World Photos*)

One of the clambakes that the Kennedys held every summer to honor the matriarch's birthday. Mrs. Kennedy is standing with her granddaughter Kathleen Kennedy (left) and daughter Eunice Shriver (right). (*AP/ Wide World Photos*)

Another clambake at Hyannis Port . . . notice the huge throng on the lawn. That's Ted to the left of Mrs. Kennedy, granddaughter Kara and daughter Pat Lawford to the right. (*UPI/Bettmann Newsphotos*)

This is the way I always think of Rose Kennedy: her arms full of flowers (including her favorite "infant's breath"), hatted, coiffed, and bejeweled (even on this casual occasion), and her head held high as she meets the public. (*AP/Wide World Photos*)

6

Hyannis Port

Returning to Hyannis Port in the spring felt like going home. After spending the winter in that big but dreary house in Palm Beach—which struck me as being the perfect setting for a Tennessee Williams play with the theme of pathetic loss and deterioration—it was an absolute pleasure to get back to the lovely white clapboard house overlooking Nantucket Sound. Thanks to the devoted efforts of Mrs. Kennedy's nephew Joe Gargan, the house was always in immaculate condition when Mrs. Kennedy arrived: floors shining with wax, new paint inside and out, freshly washed curtains stiff with starch at the sparkling windows. The rooms were open and airy, attractively decorated in light colors and floral prints, and very, very comfortable.

Mrs. Kennedy, who had spent nearly fifty summers as the mistress of this oceanfront house, had her own little routines that never varied from one year to the next. Her first order of business, as soon as she arrived in May, was the flowers that would be planted around the rambling twelve-bedroom house. This project customarily took hours and hours of planning. Mrs. Kennedy summoned her retired gardener, Wilbert Marsh, for high-level conversations, and she also consulted Alex Johnson, a local landscaper whose men would do much of the work. Finally she settled down to give orders to Arthur, the present gardener (and man of all work).

Mrs. Kennedy was very particular about how she wanted the plantings to look, especially in regard to color. She demanded that the flowers set out in the big wooden window boxes on the porch should match the shade of the curtains in the dining room as well as the paper in the entry hall! And she was always complaining that the reds weren't deep enough, the purples too dark, the pinks not as strong as she expected. She wanted her flowers to look exactly the way they did in the luscious four-color garden catalogs. The beds along the driveway and on the far side of the house, near the tennis court, did look lovely in the summer, ablaze with glorious color, with special emphasis on the brilliant pinks that were her favorites. And every year the pink roses, thriving on sea air, put on a magnificent display against the white fence. She liked to use all the flowers in arrangements for the house, and for that reason always ordered Arthur to plant copious quantities of what she called "infant's breath." I never knew whether she genuinely got the name wrong or just thought it sounded somehow more dignified than talking about baby's breath.

During my first acquaintance with that Hyannis Port house in 1968, while Joe Kennedy was still alive, it was the busy center of Kennedy family life. Even though he spent most of his time in his bedroom, his forceful personality pervaded the atmosphere. He had loved the turmoil of a big family, the continual activity it created, the warmth of family life even when it heated up into a clash—and the house was an extension of his vivid presence. But by 1974 the house had changed, in reflection of the personality of the octogenarian Rose Kennedy. It was dominated by routine, orderly and organized, and was somewhat closed to social activity. During the years I worked for Mrs. Kennedy, she erected more and more barriers between herself and the frenetic flow of family life around her.

One barrier was her edict against other people's use of the tennis court. She sent memos to the other Kennedy houses, warning against losing valuable tennis balls. One day she asked

me to tell Maria Shriver that she should use her own tennis court at home instead of coming to her grandmother's, because she brought friends with her—naturally, you can't play tennis alone—and Mrs. Kennedy didn't like to have "strangers" around the property. She seemed equally resistant to the use of her pool (like the one in Florida, Olympic-size and heated). One morning Rory and Doug Kennedy, Ethel's youngest children, turned up in my office and said they wanted to talk to their grandmother, so I buzzed her on the intercom and put them on the phone. Rory asked if they could swim in her pool, and Mrs. Kennedy answered firmly, "No, dear." She later told me that she didn't want any accidents.

Another barrier was the prohibition Mrs. Kennedy issued against the use of the movie room in the basement of her house. It had been installed by Joe Kennedy back in the late 1920s, when he still had a financial interest in the movie business. It was a scaled-down version of a real theater, complete with projection room and rows of theater seats bolted to the floor. It had for decades been a custom for the family to gather there after dinner to see a current movie. But Mrs. Kennedy was distressed by the fact that soft-drink bottles and junk-food wrappers were sometimes left behind. So she decreed that no more movies would be shown.

Gradually, fewer and fewer members of the family stopped by "Grandma's house." The older children were away for the summer or wrapped up in their own lives; the younger children took care to remain out of sight; even the adults were discouraged by the prohibitions. Mrs. Kennedy was left in peace to pursue her established daily routine. Oh, there were slight differences between Palm Beach and Hyannis Port. She read the *Cape Cod Times* instead of the shiny sheet; rather than going to St. Edward's, she attended morning mass at the simple New England church of St. Xavier's, with the altar the Kennedys had given in memory of Joe Jr.; her evening walk might take her over to the local golf course rather than along the shores of Lake Worth. But the schedule was the same. The daily menu was the same. The security of the routine was the same.

Yet Hyannis Port always brought a certain sense of informality that was missing elsewhere. Mrs. Kennedy dressed more casually, in old slacks and her orthopedic shoes. She washed and set her own hair most of the time, and, in fact, it often didn't matter what her hair looked like because she covered it with a big scarf to protect her against the strong winds of the Cape. No wonder tourists sometimes stopped her to ask the way to the Kennedy compound. She did indeed look like someone's faithful servant or impoverished relative when she got bundled up in her usual walking attire of a heavy sweater and grandmotherly babushka. It never fazed her when people did approach her, and sometimes she brought amazed tourists back to the house with her, posing for snapshots on the front lawn and graciously signing autographs. Once she got on a tour bus and rode with the crowd right up to her front door.

For me, it was always such a relief to get back to Hyannis Port. The Palm Beach house was always either too lonely or too crowded. One day Mrs. Kennedy and I were rattling around in that big shabby house by ourselves, and the next there was utter chaos because of the throngs of visiting relatives. In Hyannis Port, there were always people around, but generally they did not disturb Mrs. Kennedy's daily routine. Her health and her spirits were better there, and that made my job much easier.

I also liked Hyannis Port better because my office was so much more comfortable than the one in Palm Beach. It was a sunny room in the hallway of the main floor of the house, just off the foot of the stairs. Nearby, a hall door led outside to the pool and garage, so people were often coming and going. My office had a second door that opened onto the bright and cheery sun-room, and as long as the Kennedys weren't using it, I could keep the door open to give myself more light and space. The furniture in my office was comfortable and practical, and the walls were decorated with interesting paintings and photographs. My favorite item was the painting the Senator had done during his long convalescence from the injuries received when the small plane in which he was campaigning with Senator Birch

Bayh crashed in 1964. The painting showed the Hyannis Port waterfront, with all the Kennedy houses charmingly pictured. Its colors were bright, the spirit was cheerful, and the whole effect rather amusing and entertaining. Just being in that office made me feel more relaxed.

I thought Mrs. Kennedy, too, seemed more relaxed when she was on the Cape. Sometimes she sat down at the piano and played just for the fun of it, with particular attention to her specialty, "Sweet Adeline," played with lots of trills. She liked to sing, too. Once, when Bob Luddington, the decorator from Jordan Marsh, came to the house on an errand, he was perplexed by the cacophony coming from the kitchen. "What's *that*?" he asked me curiously. "That's Mrs. Kennedy and the cook singing in the kitchen," I answered. Their favorite was "Danny Boy," with heavy emphasis on the sad parts. The two old women had a high old time together.

Oddly enough, these high spirits were rarely in evidence during the big family get-togethers of the summer season. The Kennedys always convened to celebrate July 22, Rose Kennedy's birthday, and Labor Day, which included a birthday party for the oldest grandson, Ethel's son Joe, born several weeks later on September 24. (Interestingly, at least four other grand children, including two of Ethel's girls, had birthdays that were much closer to Labor Day, but the big party over that weekend was always in honor of Joe's birthday.) For the rest of the family, these parties were a time of family solidarity, an eagerly antic- ipated chance for immersion in a sea of Kennedy faces. For the matriarch of the clan, the events themselves seemed more like royal duties than private fun.

Mrs. Kennedy's children planned her birthday festivities, which usually included a traditional Cape Cod clambake with the whole family in attendance. But for Mrs. Kennedy, the excitement was often just too much, and she would be sick in bed for several days afterward. In 1977, the whole thing got so confused that no one knew what was supposed to happen when. The people who had been hired to cater the clambake drove up late Saturday afternoon in a truck full of lobster pots already on the boil, but none of the family showed up until after ten o'clock that night. Apparently Eunice had made a mistake and told people the affair would be on Sunday rather than Saturday, and so the whole family had merrily gone on with their usual plans until they began to get frantic phone calls about the unattended clambake. The food was long since cold and the fire completely out before most of the guests arrived, and of course Mrs. Kennedy was exhausted. Ted was angry with his sister about this mix-up and its effect on his mother, and Jackie later commented that she thought the family should have their own circus and leave Mrs. Kennedy out of it.

The Labor Day weekend was usually a more successful social event. It really got started the week before, as the grandchildren started coming in from their various summer activities in Europe, South America, Hawaii, and Indian reservations in the western states. As I looked out the windows of Mrs. Kennedy's house, I saw groups of young people walking around the yard, heading down to the beach, going back and forth between the houses, on their way to the tennis court or the swimming pool. Day by day the crowd increased, and every time I looked out I glimpsed another familiar face I hadn't seen since the previous summer. By Labor Day itself, the compound looked like a public park that was hosting a three-day outing. No wonder they don't make friends with outsiders, I thought; there are enough Kennedys to make a good party anytime.

Young Joe's birthday party was masterminded by his mother. Ethel had all the furniture on the ground floor of her house removed and the rugs rolled up to make space for the crowd. There was cold beer on tap, huge pots of chili, grilled hamburgers and hot dogs, maybe some cold boiled lobster. Later, on the tennis court, a six-piece band played for dancing, and the crowd of Kennedys all seemed to enjoy themselves.

But it was Mrs. Kennedy's custom to stay in her bedroom in her own house for much of the evening, allowing the grandchildren to pay formal visits, one at a time, to tell her about their summer activities. She seemed impressed by the social awareness of this generation. "When my children were young," she told me, "they went to far-off places to learn the culture and meet people in the government. But these children are really concerned with the social problems of the people in the countries they visit."

Early in the evening, Mrs. Kennedy would make her ritual appearance on the arm of her son Ted on one side and young Joe on the other, looking like a frail doll between these two large and solid males. It was never long before she slipped away again, back to the peace of her own house.

At least in Hyannis Port Mrs. Kennedy had a lovely bedroom to serve as her retreat. As in Palm Beach, her room was located on the second floor, right over the main entry to the house. But there the similarity ended. In Palm Beach, I couldn't understand how she managed to spend so much time in a room that was so shabby; but her bedroom in Hyannis Port was a comfortable and homey refuge. It was decorated in shades of pink, with accents of light mint green. The windows were outlined in a foam of crisp white eyelet through which the summer sun easily penetrated to keep the room bright and cheerful. The view of the ocean was of course superb. Mrs. Kennedy could look out the window as she made her daily phone calls relaying instructions to the cook in the kitchen, to me in the office, and to family members in the nearby houses. Often she worked at her desk, an antique lady's secretary with the smooth glow of well-polished old wood. Taped to the top of the desk, facing her at eye level, were mass cards commemorating the lost Kennedys: Joe, Joe Jr., Jack, Bobby, and Kathleen. She had added a few treasured snapshots, such as one of Joe Jr. in his navy uniform and one of Jack visiting his Irish relatives in the early fall of 1963. In Hyannis Port, the memories ran especially deep.

From this airy command post, Mrs. Kennedy's orders flew thick and fast. "Buy a magnifying glass for Eunice. She borrowed mine and never brought it back." "Arrange for Arthur to drive Mrs. Lawford to Boston tomorrow." "Check on the condition of the pillows in the garage apartment." "Write a memo to New York about the young woman Ethel hired to house-sit for the winter. She is apparently escorting friends around the compound, peering in the windows of Jackie's house, and so on. It seems that Ethel found her through a newspaper ad." (Later, everyone had reason to be thankful for the presence of the house-sitter, who spotted and called the Fire Department about a small fire that might well have burned the compound down if it had been unattended.)

When the telephone intercom was inadequate for her communication, Mrs. Kennedy would simply walk to the head of the stairs and call down to my ground-floor office in that carrying voice with her unmistakable Boston accent. Sometimes she also threw down papers she wanted me to take care of: clippings from her newspaper reading, notes for her book of sayings, words she wanted to know the definition of, a handwritten note she wanted me to send. I would scurry around the bottom of the stairs and frantically try to pick up the cascading papers while she stood at the top and issued a steady stream of instructions.

As in Palm Beach, however, many of Mrs. Kennedy's instructions were not followed by the household staff. Jeannette, the maid of all work, had managed to issue her own set of instructions that her employer was forced to follow. For example, it was an accepted rule that Jeannette could never be disturbed in the afternoons when she was watching her favorite soap operas. As I had learned, it was also a rule that she would never wait on other staff members, and it was a rule that she wouldn't cook for anyone but Mrs. Kennedy. One day I learned of another rule when I overheard Mrs. Kennedy, passing through the kitchen on her way to her late-afternoon walk, say apologetically to Jeannette, "I didn't have time to straighten my room yet, I'll do it when I return." It made me wonder about the conversations the two of them had at night when everyone else was gone. Jeannette was obviously more successful in issuing ultimatums than was Mrs. Kennedy.

One of Jeannette's most faithfully observed rules was that she would not stay in the house when any of the Lawfords were there. For reasons she never made entirely clear to me, she disliked the entire family so much that she arranged to go on vacation the minute the Lawfords entered the house, and she wouldn't return to work until she was sure they were gone. Since the Lawford family didn't have a house of their own on the Cape but always stayed with Mrs. Kennedy, this rule created an ongoing problem. Some summers I managed to get Nellie to come up from Florida and do the cooking. Or Pat Lawford would bring her own cook (who otherwise was expected to take an unpaid vacation whenever her employer was away). Jean Smith was always very good about bringing a maid with her, and if her own didn't come, she would hire and pay for the extra household help herself. She said cheerfully, "I know Mother doesn't like to spend money, but I do!" At least in Hyannis Port, the servant problem was never such a crisis as it was in Palm Beach. If there was no one to cook at Mrs. Kennedy's house, guests could simply go eat with Ethel or Eunice or Teddy or Jackie.

But there were times when the lack of a maid was really felt. One of the funniest was when Governor Brendan Byrne of New Jersey came to visit Mrs. Kennedy. He was attending a meeting in Hyannis and had arranged to pay a courtesy call one Friday afternoon at four o'clock. No one heard the car drive in, so one of the governor's assistants came in the back way to tell me they had arrived. I zipped round to the front door, introduced myself as Mrs. Kennedy's secretary, Barbara, and settled the governor and his two aides in the sun-room while I tried to get things organized. It turned out that Mrs. Kennedy was still getting dressed, and Jeannette was nowhere to be found . . . until I had the idea of looking in her bedroom, where I found her peacefully napping. I woke her and told her about the situation, but she refused to get up; her uniform was dirty, she said, and she wasn't going to serve. I went back downstairs to do it myself.

Mrs. Kennedy had meanwhile made her entrance, dressed to the nines in an outfit that included a matching hat. When I asked if anyone would like something to drink, Mrs. Kennedy responded by calling me "Janet" (her version of Jeannette)—as if that would turn me into a proper maid! When I was in the kitchen making iced tea and pouring some glasses of cola, Jeannette finally came out to help. She was worried that all we had was sugar-free cola, so she took matters into her own hands and added saccharine tablets to the soft drinks. "This will make it taste like real Coke," she said happily. As I passed the cold drinks, I noticed the governor looking at me with an odd expression, no doubt trying to figure out whether I was Barbara the secretary or Jeannette the maid. But his expression was nothing compared to the looks on the faces of his two aides drinking the saccharine-spiked colas.

As they left, I noticed one of them staring at Ethel's house. She had a group of college students doing some painting, and curtains were flying out the window and furniture was strewn all over the yard. I would love to know what those men said about their visit to the Kennedy compound as they drove away.

Experiences like this virtually guaranteed that Mrs. Kennedy received fewer and fewer guests as time went by. It was Ethel's house, not Grandma's, that was the real center of activity in Hyannis Port. Ethel entertained constantly. Even though there were nine bedrooms in the house, she never had enough space. Her garage had been converted into a two-bedroom apartment, and then she expanded into the little building at the rear of Jackie's yard that had formerly been used by the Secret Service. One Saturday morning I even saw guests coming out of the little dollhouse built for Ethel's children to play in; I discovered that it held a pair of twin beds for the overflow!

Later that morning I told Mrs. Kennedy about the amusing sight and she giggled, then she was silent for a moment and sighed, "The poor child." Mrs. Kennedy attributed Ethel's desire to surround herself with people to her attempt to deal with the loss of Bobby, and she never ceased to feel sympathetic about the cause of Ethel's actions, even if she was sometimes inconvenienced by their results.

If you went into Ethel's home by the front entrance, you had to contend with the sagging and rotted porch floor and the Kennedy children climbing on the porch roof and occasionally dropping water bombs on passersby. If you went in the back entrance, you stumbled over huge boxes of groceries just delivered from the market, giant piles of laundry waiting to be washed, and a bunch of children telling the cook what they wanted to eat. There were no set hours for daytime meals; people just turned up when they were hungry and told the cook what they wanted. Following the custom established long ago by Bobby, at night everyone ate together at the dining room table: children, governesses, secretaries, visiting relatives, and famous guests.

And the famous guests were, more often than not, on hand. Ethel's houseguests included athletes like Rafer Johnson, Bruce Jenner, Rosie Grier; columnist Art Buchwald and TV journalist Barbara Walters; singer Andy Williams and comic Buddy Hackett; the beautiful Farrah Fawcett and the folksy David Hartman. These famous faces drifted around the compound, playing tennis on Mrs. Kennedy's court, walking across her lawn to get to the beach, sometimes stopping in to pay their respects to the matriarch of the family. Art Buchwald created a bit of a stir by taking the Kennedy kids to a nude beach. (Ted's younger son, Patrick, later reported he had been too embarrassed to look.) Buddy Hackett didn't like boats, but preferred to stay inside and cook (especially chili). Rafer was an enthusiastic sailor. It was fun to watch the comings and goings of these glamorous visitors.

The doings at Ethel's house could be counted on to provide entertainment. I always got a kick out of watching Ethel handle her large volume of correspondence. She would lie on a comfortable chaise in her front yard, redolent of suntan oil, stretched out in her bathing suit to get the full benefit of the sun. Her secretary would be sitting next to her, fully dressed, bolt upright on a chair, feverishly scribbling away.

Most of Ethel's employees didn't last long; the demands of that large and lively household simply ground them down. There was at least one new cook every summer—sometimes two or three. She hired many of them fresh out of a cooking school in Virginia, but their newly learned skills were rarely adequate to the demands of working for Ethel Kennedy. The cook literally fixed meals all day long, from early morning until late at night. One of these young men told my son, "Every night I go home and change my clothes and go out to the nearest bar and stay until they close. The next morning, when I wake up, I sit in the shower for about forty-five minutes. It takes all that time to get me in here to face this every morning." Jackie once painted a picture as a present for Ethel, depicting the house with children running in and out, hanging out of the upstairs windows, playing on the roof. One cook is trudging out the back door, clothes askew and hair untidy, head down and hastily packed suitcase in hand. Simultaneously, through the front door strides the new cook, neatly dressed and looking hopeful and confident. One thing I always liked about Ethel is that she thought the picture was as funny as everyone else did.

Perhaps it was that aspect of Ethel's personality that made people congregate at her house. You could often find the Shriver children there, having a snack or an extra meal. Jackie's children, Caroline and John, headed there as soon as they got to Hyannis Port, to see their cousins and catch up on all the news. There was always something going on at Ethel's because she liked to keep herself busy. She played a lot of tennis and she loved to sail. Every day Ethel had the cook of the moment prepare huge lunch hampers, filled with sandwiches, deviled eggs, roast chicken, lobster, cheese, fruit, cookies, cold soft drinks, and beer and wine; Mrs. Kennedy called this Ethel's "movable feast." Around noon, she would sweep up everyone in sight—children, house-guests, miscellaneous friends, my son Kevin when he was with me for the summer—and they would go off on one of her sail-boats for a few hours. If by chance she happened to forget the dogs (a pair of spaniels that seemed to enjoy sailing), she would stop the boat and they would jump in the water and swim out, where someone would haul them onto the boat.

One memorable day the movable feast came to grief. It was not long before Labor Day, and an unusually large crowd had turned up at the pier at noon to go out on the boat with Ethel. Arthur happened to be outside as they were embarking and he later told me at least twenty-five had boarded the sloop. "They'll never make it," he predicted. As it turned out, he was right. Luckily they weren't too far from shore when the boat capsized; several people spotted the mishap and all on board were quickly picked up. The boat, hampers and all, sank right down to the bottom, like a toy in a bathtub—only this was a $65,000 toy. (The boat was eventually refloated.) Afterward, houseguest Buddy Hackett congratulated himself on his foresight in having decided to stay behind in Ethel's kitchen to whip up a batch of chili.

Part of the chaos at Ethel's house was due to the large canine population. I remember that in the summer of 1977, Ethel had eight dogs: the spaniels, a whippet, some little dogs that looked like animated dust mops, and a pair of big black dogs that loved to bark and jump up on people. One night that summer, one of the big dogs attacked Mrs. Kennedy. She told me about the incident the next morning. "My dear, he had me on the ground." Her dress was all dirty and her hip was bruised; the cook told me that when she came in afterward, her teeth were chattering from the fright it had given her. I don't think the dog meant to harm her, but it was big and enthusiastic, and she was small and frail, and the outcome was inevitable. Really, I was surprised that it happened only once. Everyone in the neighborhood complained about those dogs, and I always felt that they were one of the riskier aspects of going to Ethel's house.

The contrast between Ethel's household and Jackie's, located just a few hundred yards away, was enormous. At Jackie's house, things always seemed to be peaceful and well organized. Whenever I had occasion to go there, I usually found the same scene: a house so quiet I thought perhaps no one was home, Jackie enjoying the sun on her very private deck or stretched out on the porch sofa with a good book in her hand and a cold drink by her side. She came to Hyannis Port for a vacation, and unlike the rest of the Kennedy family, she actually seemed to be able to relax.

Another way Jackie was different was her thoughtfulness about the people who worked for her. She arranged summer schedules so that each of her domestic staff would have a chance to be in Hyannis Port for a few weeks of sun and ocean air. They were even urged to bring along their children. One day I found the maid's baby gurgling happily in a playpen that had been set up in the kitchen. And Jackie was always careful to tip all the local people who helped her out. For example, she gave Arthur a generous tip at the end of the season for tending her lawn and garden. Although he also did yard work for Ethel, as well as Ted and Eunice when he had the time, none of them ever thought of offering him something extra for his trouble.

Several times Jackie asked me to help her out with some typing. The first time, I assumed it would be like the work I did for the other members of the family, for which I usually received only a "thank you." But when I finished the work for Jackie—typing up some pages of Russian translation for a book she was working on at Doubleday—I was surprised to receive in return a handwritten note of thanks along with a check for a generous sum, hand-delivered immediately by her butler. No wonder everyone knocked themselves out for Jackie.

It was impossible to ignore the glamour that surrounded Jacqueline Kennedy Onassis, and yet she herself never gave any sign that she was aware of it. I remember the first fall I worked for Mrs. Kennedy, when Jackie called me one day. She always stayed on the Cape longer than the rest of the family, taking particular pleasure in the quiet autumn days. She had called to check on whether Mrs. Kennedy had gotten off to Paris on schedule the day before, and I described the rather frenzied departure. Then we got to talking about the strain of these long trips on Mrs. Kennedy's health, and her admirable desire to keep up her usual activities as long as she was able. Jackie said with affectionate amusement, "You wouldn't believe what Grandma goes through with the saleswomen and fitters when she buys her clothes from a French couturier." Apparently Mrs. Kennedy was an absolute perfectionist about fit, outdoing the standards of even the most meticulous employees. Suddenly I realized we had been on the phone for nearly half an hour, just chatting in a casual way. I found Jackie to be a very private person, who preferred to remain uninvolved with all the daily crises of life in the Kennedy compound. But she was never aloof, never unfriendly. She was either absent altogether, or she was totally present: open, interested, responsive.

As I thought about Jackie, Ethel, and Rose Kennedy, it

struck me that the famous Kennedy compound had turned into a matriarchal society. In the 1950s and '60s, the presiding spirit of the place had been relentlessly masculine, created by the highly competitive Joe Kennedy and his equally competitive sons Jack and Bobby. Those were the days of the much-chronicled football games, played with a cutthroat determination to win; of the sailboat races that also had to be won rather than merely enjoyed; of dinner conversation that was as competitive as any sport; of guests who were powerful figures in the world of international affairs. But now the ethos of the compound was created by the three widows whose houses seemed to cluster together for support. Kennedys were no longer winning races but sinking their sailboats offshore. Guests, however charming, were merely famous, never powerful, and often no longer even active in the careers that had brought them into the public eye. The glories of the past were obviously fading.

It was then that I realized how formidable the loss of Rose's husband had been. With Ted rarely present, the Kennedy compound was desperate for a masculine presence. Someone to demand that the domestic staff stay on its toes and to let loose a few colorful curses when that didn't happen. Someone to make the children and the dogs behave by occasionally throwing a little fear into them. And all the husbands were missed. Those three lonely women needed someone to bring them out from behind the defenses they had spent years constructing.

I remember that one day a neighbor called to complain about the problems caused by the steady stream of curious tourists who wanted to see the Kennedy compound. The influx posed a security threat to the neighborhood, she said, and she thought something ought to be done about it. She demanded to speak to whoever was "in charge." Ruefully, I realized that her request summed up the problem of the compound: There was no one in charge. Life went on, children dashed around the place, adults entertained guests, repairs to the property eventually got made, the big Labor Day party was held one more time. But as I watched all this going on around me, I always thought it was like the good ship *Lollipop* without a captain: Even though it looked like a good time was being had by all, they were only going around and around in circles.

Ted Kennedy tried to fill the vacuum. He would scoop up everyone in sight and take them out on his yawl for an afternoon of real sailing. Or he would stop by to see his mother and inject much-needed warmth and laughter into her otherwise rather cloistered existence. He would take the boys out fishing and proudly return with a big one to cook for dinner. He loved children (Mrs. Kennedy told me he had always wanted a big family like Bobby's) and he enjoyed playing uncle. Once he drove gaily into the compound driveway in a Winnebago camper he had rented for a week and, like the Pied Piper, gathered all the children he could find to take them on a trip to Maine. (Subsequent reports from some of the children indicated that he had also stopped in Boston to pick up a girlfriend to go along on the trip.)

But there was more than any one man could do. He had inherited his brothers' weighty political legacy as well as the position of head of the family and father figure to seventeen nieces and nephews made fatherless by death or divorce. And all this was on top of his own concerns with his career, his presidential aspirations, his marriage in crisis, his three children to care for—Ted Jr. with his leg lost to bone cancer, Patrick with such severe asthma that oxygen tanks were kept in the house, and Kara in her teens with the usual problems about her own identity. It was too much to expect of any one man that he could handle all of those roles and fill all those needs by himself.

So we drifted on. It was easy to see why Mrs. Kennedy chose to remain isolated within her own home: The surrounding confusion and chaos were too much for her. Sometimes they were too much for me! There was the day I had to go to the Hyannis airport to meet Ethel's private plane. It turned out that I was one of a sizable convoy. It took several vehicles to load up the children, the dogs, the luggage, the sports equipment, the maids, a coffeepot, flower arrangements from a dinner party the night before, all of which came out of the plane like clowns out of a circus car. Ethel never believed in traveling light; even when she came to Florida for a visit of a week or so, she arrived with mounds of luggage. The turmoil involved in getting that family from the airport to their house was unbelievable.

Perhaps even more unbelievable was the problem involved in getting the Shrivers *to* the airport. Eunice called one morning and asked if I could drive her and her sons Mark and Anthony to the airport in Mrs. Kennedy's car. I explained that she would be using it to go to mass at noon, so Eunice suggested that I drive to their house in my own car and then use their old 1960 Lincoln to transport them all. "Can we leave here at twelve-twenty?" she pressed. I agreed.

I arrived at the Shrivers at twelve-ten only to find that Eunice was just getting into the shower. She told me to wait in the living room, but the house was so dirty I didn't want to sit down. When she finally appeared, I handed her a pile of copies of *Times to Remember*, the book of Mrs. Kennedy's memoirs published in 1974, which Maria had left for her grandmother to autograph. "Do you want to pack these with your things?" I asked.

"Can't you mail these yourself?" she replied. "I have a million things to do and I can't take care of everything. Just call my secretary in Washington and get the addresses," she ordered. Then she added, "Do you think you can do this without bothering Mother?" I smiled ruefully at her version of "Don't tell Mother."

We all got into the car and set out, but hadn't traveled more than a few blocks when the car had a flat tire. It was obvious that the question of what to do next was up to me; Eunice seemed to be waiting for me to solve the problem single-handedly. I could have walked back to get my car, but it was too small to hold all the people and luggage crowded into the big Lincoln. So I boldly approached a woman I could see pulling out of her driveway and asked her to take everyone to the airport. She was surprised, but she eventually agreed. I walked back to Mrs. Kennedy's and called a garage to fix the tire. They later reported that it was in shreds and that the spare was also unusable, so I told them to put on a retread and send the Shrivers the bill. After work, I walked back to the house to pick up my own car and to check that the garage had returned Eunice's car, as promised. I found all the doors and windows open, just as if the residents had only gone next door for a few minutes. They had left the house until the following spring and not even bothered to close the front door.

Experiences like this made life at Mrs. Kennedy's house seem positively normal. Well, almost. . . . By now I took it in my stride when Mrs. Kennedy announced that we were going to straighten up the attic. It no longer bothered me that we had been doing this afternoon after afternoon for four years in a row. At first it had simply seemed silly, because the attic was perfectly neat. But I finally realized it was Mrs. Kennedy's way of revisiting the past and perhaps also coming to terms with it, and it was more important to her than answering letters from strangers. So I stopped worrying about the correspondence and spent the time the way it mattered to my employer.

And, of course, poking around the attic was always fascinating. There were pieces of antique furniture and collections of old china. There were two large cedar-lined closets that Mr. and Mrs. Kennedy had used for storage of evening clothes, hats and shoes, things like the soft velvet hat the Ambassador had worn when he got an honorary degree from President Eamon De Valera of Ireland. Trophies and awards and commendations that were not important enough to hang in the house but too meaningful to throw away were neatly stored in the attic. One day we found several forgotten treasures: one of Toscanini's batons in a glass case, and a frame that held a plate that had been used by George Washington, along with a lock of his hair. (We got that out and hung it in the dining room: it was later appraised at $3,000.)

Best of all were the old letters, postcards, scrapbooks. It seemed that Kathleen especially had been a great one for keeping memorabilia, and the attic contained her old dance programs, albums of snapshots, newspaper clippings about her friends, even letters that she had written her family in the sadly brief period between the time of her marriage and the battlefront

death of her husband during World War II. There were also letters from Jack Kennedy to his parents that dated back to his wartime service in the South Pacific. I was afraid these might be upsetting to Mrs. Kennedy, but when she read them, she began to laugh in appreciation of Jack's wit and quite enjoyed these messages from the past, many of which he had jokingly signed with the pseudonym "Betty Blitch."

The attic even contained scrapbooks that dated back to the time Rose Fitzgerald was a high school girl and her father was the mayor of Boston. The distant past was vividly alive for her, and she was careful to keep up with the few friends from that period who were still living.

One of them, Marie Greene, came for lunch one day. The two women had been estranged for several years after biographer Gail Cameron interviewed Mrs. Greene for her book *Rose*, and Mrs. Greene said of Mrs. Kennedy's mother, "Josie, of course, was a bitch." But somehow the old friends had reconciled, and Mrs. Kennedy was in high spirits as she waited to greet her guest. She looked wonderful, dressed in one of her designer outfits complete with big hat. As soon as Mrs. Greene arrived, they went into the bright and cheerful sun-room, with its alcove decorated with hundreds of family photos. I figured the flow of reminiscence would be fast and furious, but when I went in to tell them lunch was ready, I found Mrs. Greene working very slowly on finishing an interminable sentence, while Mrs. Kennedy was looking as if she were about to fall asleep. I waited for Mrs. Greene to grind to a halt, but she gave no sign of doing so in my lifetime. Eventually I decided I had no choice but to interrupt. Mrs. Greene gave no sign she had heard me and simply continued talking. Mrs. Kennedy, wearing a rather martyred expression, was staring fixedly at the ceiling. The cook later told me that the lunch went on in the same way, and that she had spent twenty minutes waiting for Mrs. Greene to answer the question of whether she wanted coffee, tea, or Sanka. When Mrs. Greene finally left, Mrs. Kennedy came into my office and sighed. "I thought I was in a bad way . . . she really is stupid!"

We laughed together, but I could tell Mrs. Kennedy was proud that she was more vigorous and attractive than most other women her age.

She also maintained a busier public schedule than her contemporaries. She was frequently interviewed by the local press. She appeared, with other members of the family, at the dedication ceremonies at the Kennedy Library. Richard Avedon took her photograph for *Rolling Stone*—unfortunately on a day that she was in a bad mood. She had asked me to stay with her to help, to be sure her dress was properly arranged and to remind her to keep her hands out of sight, since she thought they were the one feature that really betrayed her age. But during the shooting session, she changed her mind and suddenly announced, "Barbara, please leave the room. You're distracting me." The picture that appeared in the magazine was shot almost immediately afterward. Everything is there in her face for the world to see: her anger, her desire to be the eternal center of attention, and all the pain she has suffered.

Part of Mrs. Kennedy's public schedule was campaigning for her son in her native state of Massachusetts. During Ted's 1976 campaign for reelection to the Senate, she made several appearances on his behalf. One was a reception on Cape Cod, in nearby Falmouth. As she was dressing, she asked me to call Eunice, who was supposed to accompany her, to see whether or not she was ready. I admitted that I had just seen Eunice and Ethel walk by on their way to the tennis court. Mrs. Kennedy was obviously worried, and when Eunice bounded upstairs ten minutes later, I had the feeling the discussion was far from pleasant. A few minutes later, Mrs. Kennedy came downstairs, looking smashing in a floor-length blue chiffon dress embroidered with silver medallions. She stood in the entry hall and suddenly hiked up her dress to adjust her underwear. "Those two ninnies," she said, "are out on the tennis court when they should be doing this. After all, I'm eighty-six years old!" Just then Ethel turned up, miraculously dressed in that short time and also looking very nice. I heard later that Mrs. Kennedy was the hit of the reception. She told the audience, "It's all right to go campaigning when you are sixty-six, or even seventy-six. But when you get to be eighty-six it is a little too much. Don't let your children do that to you!" Everyone laughed and applauded.

Despite—or perhaps because of—her heavier public schedule in Hyannis Port, Mrs. Kennedy usually seemed happier when we were on the Cape. I felt much the same way. Since the house was in good repair and we had few houseguests, household crises were at a minimum. And when problems did arise, there were members of the family around to intervene. Compared to Palm Beach, Hyannis Port was practically a vacation, and I was always sorry when it was time to leave in the fall.

I never could decide whether to laugh or cry over Mrs. Kennedy's departure. The moment itself was the picture of propriety. While the car waited in the driveway to take her to the Boston airport, the staff assembled on the wide front porch to tell her good-bye. Jeannette, Arthur, myself, and perhaps Joe Gargan and one or two other people lined up to kiss her good-bye and wave to her as she disappeared down the driveway; this was the staff ritual, so her children never participated. Then the minute she was out of sight, everyone rushed away with unseemly haste. (Their pay stopped as soon as their employer left.) Jeannette was so anxious to leave that while she was standing on the porch waving good-bye, she had her car idling in the back driveway and the door on the driver's side standing open so she wouldn't waste a precious second before she zoomed away.

It was just one more example of the difference between the storybook appearance of life with the Kennedys and the reality.

7

A Matter of Money

When it came to matters of money, I always felt Mrs. Kennedy's attitude could only be described as eccentric.

There was no question that the Kennedy family was indeed very wealthy. Recent estimates put the total family holdings at somewhere close to half a billion dollars. In the recently published *The Very Rich Book*, Jacqueline Thompson says there are only ten families in the entire country whose amalgamated net worth exceeds the Kennedys'.

But, while Mrs. Kennedy could at times behave like the woman of great wealth that she was, at other times she was more like an ordinary housewife on a restricted budget. Her respect for thrift probably stemmed from her relatively less affluent childhood and was compounded by her simple inexperience with matters of money. Like many widows of her generation, she had an Old World sense of economy that had never been relaxed because her husband had always handled all expenditures. She had no experience in making money or in deciding how to spend it, and so her inclination was to save it when she could. Like many wealthy people, Mrs. Kennedy would spend appropriately for what she considered "necessary luxuries," but would be more careful with nonessential expenditures. But, unlike others of her class, Mrs. Kennedy had what I felt was a very peculiar and severe idea of what was necessary and what was not.

For instance, every year she sent all her distant relatives large checks for Christmas, and she was unfailingly generous whenever one of them was in need. But when it came to her own grandchildren, she could certainly never be accused of being the one who spoiled them. Each of the twenty-nine grand-children, even the ones who were then in their teens, got just fifteen dollars on their birthday. Exceptions to this rule were rare. One year Pat Lawford suggested that it would be nice for Mrs. Kennedy to give her godchild Victoria Lawford a portable electric typewriter for her birthday. Mrs. Kennedy responded to this suggestion with a very funny letter about the impossibility of spending such a large amount as $125. She explained that she was already going to have to spend extra money on her godchild Maria Shriver that year because it was her twenty-first birthday. She went on to remind Pat that Joe Kennedy had already given all the grandchildren a great deal of money and so she herself was not in the least concerned about them. She closed sweetly, "Much love and affection."

The mention of her children's independent wealth was just one of the ways Mrs. Kennedy honored the memory of Joe Kennedy. Years after his death, she remained devoted. She liked to talk about the days of their courtship, and she once said emphatically, "I fell in love when I was only seventeen and I never fell out!" She often spoke admiringly of his talent for making money, which she regarded with a kind of mystical awe. "He was really wonderful," she told me one day. "Why, he could make even you rich!"

But, without her husband there to guide her, Mrs. Kennedy often ended up worrying most about the smallest expenses. She would become obsessed with the idea that she was spending too much money for phone service and decide to take out some of the extensions—a convenience that cost only $6.50 a month in a house worth millions. Or she would get all fired up about making a donation to the local thrift shop, and she and I would spend hours sorting through old clothes and household goods. Then Dennis or Arthur would spend more time delivering the things to the shop. Many of the things she donated weren't even salable. The funniest example I remember was when she gave the Hyannis thrift shop *one* of Teddy's old sneakers.

One day I heard Mrs. Kennedy telling the cook not to fix her a baked potato for lunch because it would cost too much to turn on the oven to cook (this in a house where the bill for the outdoor pool was over six hundred dollars a month). Another time, when Jeannette was away and I volunteered to prepare her dinner she told me she wanted to have the baked potato left over from the day before. I was distressed because that very morning I had cleaned out the refrigerator and thrown away the wizened potato I found lying at the back of the shelf. "I've never warmed up a baked potato before," I temporized. "It's very simple," explained Pat, who was visiting at the time. "Just scoop it out and put it in a double boiler with butter, salt and pepper." So I rushed downstairs calling Arthur to come help me retrieve the potato, which I luckily found I could easily wash off and still use. Later, when I asked her how the meal had been, she answered, "Well, the lamb chop was so-so, but the potato was delicious."

When the family was visiting, Mrs. Kennedy set a bountiful table. When the Shrivers and Lawfords stayed with Mrs. Kennedy in Palm Beach over Christmas one year, the grocery bill for their eight-day stay was more than $1,700, and on top of that, there were additional large bills from the liquor store, the fish market, and the gourmet specialty store. A typical dinner menu (often planned by Sarge Shriver) might be:

Cold Vichyssoise
Shrimp Cocktail
Crown Roast of Lamb (2)
Tiny New Potatoes
Two Vegetables
Baked Alaska

Yet when the guests left after the holidays, Mrs. Kennedy decided to turn off the water cooler to save electricity. And when the water man came one time to pick up the empty ten-gallon bottles, she chided him for taking one that still had a tiny bit left. Would he please empty it into a glass so it could be drunk?

Another incident that emphasized the contrasts in spending and saving in Mrs. Kennedy's household occurred in Hyannis Port. We were paddling around in the pool, talking about this and that, and she asked me if I had remembered to order the lobster for dinner that night. She had invited some of the family over for the delightful treat of fresh boiled Maine lobster served with lots of melted butter—a luxury that cost more than fifty dollars to feed that many people. "Yes, they'll be delivered this afternoon," I said, "and I thought you might like potato chips, too, so I ordered a bag of those." She replied thoughtfully, "I believe we already have a bag in the kitchen." "Oh, well," I replied, "you can always use them." But the thought of those unneeded potato chips clearly worried Mrs. Kennedy, and a few minutes later she asked me to leave the pool and call the shop back and cancel the order for one 59-cent bag.

In fact, for some reason it was most often food that brought out Mrs. Kennedy's economical streak. I'll never forget the affair of the missing pieces of chicken. The day after chicken had been served to dinner guests in Hyannis Port, Mrs. Kennedy went into the kitchen and counted the leftover pieces in the refrigerator. She discovered she was missing two, and the fact caused an uproar. Jeannette, put on the spot because she was unable to account for the loss, suggested maybe I had eaten the missing pieces. So Mrs. Kennedy stormed into my office and exclaimed, "You took my chicken!" I had to laugh, but to satisfy my own curiosity, I did a little detective work later that day and established that the chicken in question had been appropriated as a snack by Bobby Shriver. That fact became one more of the "Don't tell Mrs. Kennedy" conspiracies.

Sometimes she would say to me, "I'd like to see the food bills . . . why don't I ever see them?" The answer, of course, was that I had been instructed by the New York office to show

Mrs. Kennedy only small bills, then approve the rest and send them on to New York. And those food bills were definitely not small! So I would just answer that I didn't know. "I ought to see them," she would insist. "I don't know what that cook is doing. She could be ordering strawberries out of season for all I know."

One reason the New York office kept those larger bills from Mrs. Kennedy was so that necessary repairs and maintenance could be done. Her reluctance to spend for that purpose had allowed the Palm Beach house to deteriorate to the point where the value of that very valuable oceanfront property was declining. Things got in such a state that in the fall of 1976, several people from the New York office went to Florida to assess the situation, decide what repairs were needed, and then hire someone to do them all. When I got to the house in early October, I found the front door missing, plaster all over the dining room, and a huge hole in the back of the garage apartment. Plumbers, electricians, sandblasters, and painters were scurrying around all corners of the house and grounds. The people who set this chaos in motion had wisely retreated to New York.

In the middle of all this uproar, Mrs. Kennedy called to say she was ready to come down—a few weeks earlier than expected—despite Jean Smith's efforts to delay her with dinner parties and luncheon guests. Of course, she knew nothing about the extensive renovations in progress. In order to finish the work before she arrived, we had to ask the various contractors to come in and work double-time over the weekend—thus unfortunately spending more money to keep her from finding out she was spending money. By the time Mrs. Kennedy arrived, everything was finished except the garage apartment, which looked like a bomb site. For the next week, Dennis, Mam'selle, and I had to make sure Mrs. Kennedy went in and out through the formal front entrance rather than the back way, which would take her right by the garage. She never noticed the repairs to the rest of the house, except to comment that everything looked very clean and fresh.

Sometimes all our subterfuge failed. For example, the big old-fashioned freezer in the Palm Beach house broke down that same fall, and I hired a man to fix it. Mrs. Kennedy walked into the back kitchen while he was at work. I had to confess what was going on and tell her the repair was going to cost a hundred dollars. I pointed out that we needed a working freezer, especially since the house would soon be full of company. "What will we do when everyone comes for Thanksgiving and Christmas?" I asked.

"We can make do with the freezer compartment of the refrigerator," she replied triumphantly.

"But there's not nearly enough space," I explained. "And this is the only place for all the ice cream that everyone eats for dessert."

"They don't need ice cream," Mrs. Kennedy shot back. "They can eat milk and cookies for dessert." I looked at her out of the corner of my eye and said, "Now, Mrs. Kennedy . . ." and she finally laughed and said, "Oh, all right," and went back upstairs to her room.

We had the same sort of problem about carpeting for the attic steps in the Hyannis Port house. They were very steep and a bit slippery and I was afraid someone would fall, perhaps Mrs. Kennedy herself. But I knew I would have to clear it with her, since she would see the carpeting. I told her I was worried about the safety hazard and added that I had even slipped on those stairs myself. Sears could carpet them for about fifty dollars, I explained. There was a silence, then, "It must be you," she said briskly. "After all, we've been here for forty years and no one else has ever fallen on those steps." No more was ever said about the carpeting.

The whole episode reminded me of a story I had heard from someone in the New York office about the time years before when Mrs. Kennedy had instructed the maid to put a low-wattage bulb in the hallway lamp to save on the electric bill. Joe Kennedy took one look at the gloomy hallway and said indignantly, "Christ, Rose, you might save a few cents a month on that light bulb, but it will cost thousands of dollars if I have to go to the hospital with a broken leg from falling in the dark."

Mrs. Kennedy's inexperienced concept of spending and saving didn't improve after her husband's death because of the peculiar role of the New York office in the family finances. The office, on the thirtieth floor of the Pan Am Building, had been set up by Joe Kennedy to manage the privately held real estate and oil companies he owned, to administer the trusts he had established for the children and grandchildren, and to operate charitable and memorial activities he had set in motion. There were about a half dozen employees in the New York office. The ever-helpful Tom Walsh was one of the key figures there, and Steve Smith was more or less at the helm. Most of the people who worked there had been hired by Joe Kennedy, and he had indoctrinated them with his policies. He had spent his life building up a fortune so that none of his children or grandchildren would ever even have to think about money. Instead, the employees of that office were the only ones who understood his tangled financial empire. The family was not to be bothered with such mundane concerns.

The New York office handled all financial transactions for Mrs. Kennedy—and for everyone else in the family, too. Fixed expenses such as taxes, mortgage and maintenance payments, insurance, and so on were automatically paid by the office when due. For other expenses, the family just had the bills sent to New York. If a Kennedy wanted to buy filet mignon or rent a car or splurge at Cartier, paying the bill was simply a matter of having it sent to the New York office. If someone in the family wanted to buy another house, they called the New York office for approval. If Mrs. Kennedy wanted to leave her brother $25,000 in her will, she called the New York office to see if she had it to leave. Kennedys who overspent eventually had the matter forcibly brought to their attention. Those like Mrs. Kennedy who underspent on maintenance had the money put out for them behind their backs.

I could understand how easy it was for all the family to leave things to the New York office, because I often did the same thing. The people who worked there were always very nice to me, particularly Tom Walsh, a fatherly sort of man who called me "darling" and did all he could to make my life easier. The first winter I went to Palm Beach with Mrs. Kennedy, I talked to Tom about finding myself an apartment to rent, since I had definitely decided I would never "live in" at Mrs. Kennedy's. "Just look around for something you like, darling," Tom advised me. "How much rent will you pay?" I asked. "Just find a place you like and let me know about it," Tom responded genially.

The same thing happened when I talked to him about leasing a car for me. Even though I was getting mileage for the driving I did in my own car, I felt that my little Duster was depreciating far too rapidly because of the number of miles I was putting on it, driving back and forth between Massachusetts and Florida and rushing around on errands like going to the airport to pick up visitors or into town on my lunch hour to buy something Mrs. Kennedy needed urgently. So I suggested to Tom that they might lease a car for me. "Of course, darling," said Tom. "How much will you pay a month?" I asked. "You just shop around and see what kind of a price you can get," answered Tom. I really didn't know whether he expected me to look at Pintos or Cadillacs, but I ended up with a wonderful little Mustang with an all-white interior and a tape deck that was the envy of all the Kennedy grandchildren. "God, Barbara, what a nice car," said Caroline after she had borrowed it one afternoon to slip past reporters. In such circumstances, it is easy to lose touch with financial realities. The New York office could take care of those for everyone.

The system was set up to protect the entire family from financial worries. The result was that none of them—Steve Smith excepted—really knew anything about how to manage money. They didn't even know how much they had. Mrs. Kennedy, who was certainly worth millions, had no idea what she could afford and what she couldn't. For example, acting in what they believed to be her best interest, the people in the New York office would tell her she couldn't afford to give so much money to relatives. Then, behind her back, the same people would authorize significant expenditures to reroof the Hyannis Port house or buy new appliances or, in my case, to pay for the services of a personal secretary to make Mrs. Kennedy's life easier. No doubt their budget decisions were correct, but the point is that these were New York's budget decisions, not Mrs. Kennedy's. More than once, she became exasperated and telephoned the New York office to demand to know how much money she had. They always said they would let her know . . . but no one ever returned the call.

This way of handling money—which I have learned is not at all uncommon in families of great wealth—tends to make people behave like children. Lacking both full knowledge and real responsibility, they are naturally unable to make sensible judgments about how much they should spend. If they spend too much or too little, indulge all their appetites or fail to buy enough food to stay alive, someone else will have to deal with the consequences.

I am sure this was partly the cause of Mrs. Kennedy's erratic spending behavior. And the more frequently that decisions about paying for necessities such as a new clothes dryer or maintenance of the pool were made behind her back, the more it must have seemed to her that she was right in taking the attitude she did. For example, in Palm Beach she had flatly refused to spend any money to fix the pool heating system. So the New York office and I conspired to have it taken care of without her knowledge. The necessary repairs were made (and her account was charged for the cost), so the heating system functioned perfectly from then on. But from Mrs. Kennedy's point of view, it must have appeared that the heating system just stopped giving trouble. Naturally, she would conclude that she was right in refusing to spend any money to have it fixed, since the problem seemed to have fixed itself. So the next time I asked her to spend money on some kind of repair or maintenance, she would be even more likely to refuse.

The contradictions that grew out of this situation continually boggled my mind. Take the matter of Mrs. Kennedy's annual trip to Paris. She always stayed in the elegant and luxurious Plaza Athenée, where she was such a dependably regular guest that the hotel even kept her belongings in storage for her from one year to the next, so she didn't have to travel back and forth with her pajamas, dressing gown, cosmetics, alarm clock, and so on. She would shop at the couturier salons, spending more than $1,000 for a dress from Jean-Louis Sherrer, $450 at Dior for blouses, $250 on a new hat. Yet in order to travel to Paris, she insisted on getting the lowest possible fare, even though that meant she would have to leave at an inconvenient time and stay away for three weeks. Of course, she flew tourist instead of first-class, and because she found the food inedible she had the cook pack her a little lunch of chicken sandwiches, her favorite cookies, and milk in a thermos to tide her over. And she wouldn't let me hire a limo to meet her; she always said she'd just take a taxi. In fact, not only did she take a taxi, she usually tried to save a little more money by sharing it with someone else waiting in the taxi line. She did that once on her arrival back in New York, and the woman was so flustered to find herself riding in a yellow cab with Rose Kennedy that she actually fainted! The driver had to stop and revive her.

One of Mrs. Kennedy's favorite economies was particularly frustrating to friends and relatives who wanted to give her presents for birthdays and Christmas. Mrs. Kennedy invariably returned presents for credit. She would deny herself, and instead use the credit to give others gifts. Teddy gave her a pretty and stylish beach coat for her birthday (or, to be more accurate, he had me pick it out and put it on his account), and she returned it for credit. Jackie gave her a lovely pair of hand-embroidered sheets from Porthault for her bedroom in Hyannis Port; her mother-in-law first asked her to exchange them for green rather than pink embroidery and then eventually returned the green ones for a credit. When Ted noticed how old her record player was (Mrs. Kennedy said merrily, "It's an antique, like everything else around here, including me!") and gave her a fancy new one, she made him return it for credit. When people sent flowers for her birthday, she asked the florist to stop delivery and give her a credit instead. This led to embarrassing situations. More than once, someone who had sent flowers dropped by to see how they looked. This called for quick thinking on my part: Since good manners forbade a vistor's invasion of Mrs. Kennedy's bedroom, I would usually claim that she had decided to put the flowers there.

I used to amuse myself by working out the complicated trail that led from one present to another. For example, Mrs. Kennedy had received a handsome picture frame from Barbara Walters as a thank-you after she visited Hyannis Port; the frame was promptly returned to Cartier for credit. A few months later, Mrs. Kennedy bought Jackie a sweet little gold pillbox for Christmas with that credit. . . . There were many similarly tangled trails.

It was a real feat of ingenuity when someone came up with a present that Mrs. Kennedy would actually keep. Jackie managed it one time by bringing back from Greece a beautiful silver crucifix to which she had tied a bright strand of ribbon so it could be hung on Mrs. Kennedy's bed; not even Mrs. Kennedy could resist such a gift. One year the children arranged to have the books written by various members of the family bound in matching leather for the bookshelves in the living room of the Hyannis Port house. Mrs. Kennedy appreciated the thought but noted that the leather didn't really match the colors of the living room. Color-coordinated or not, she kept the specially bound and stamped volumes. The grandchildren often got around the problem by asking her what she wanted for Christmas or a birthday and then simply buying whatever it was. Her requests were for such exotic items as white ankle socks (which had to be purchased in the children's department) or a new rosary or a pair of binoculars so she could keep an eye on "you people" at the pier or far corners of the yard. Of course, having asked for these gifts, Mrs. Kennedy couldn't return them, and it was most frequently in this way that the family outsmarted her and made her accept something nice for herself.

Mrs. Kennedy also frequently returned things she had bought herself, when she got home and decided she didn't really need them. Since most of the places she shopped were used to her foibles, they generally took things back without a fuss. But one day she gave me a lipstick and a bottle of nail polish remover to take back to the drugstore for credit. The clerk took a look and then protested, "But these have been used." Embarrassed, I mumbled something about Mrs. Kennedy not liking them. "Oh, really," said the clerk, "this sort of thing has been going on for years with her account." The next time she gave me used cosmetics to return, I simply threw them away and never mentioned the subject again.

Having learned my lesson from that experience, I was more cautious when one day on Worth Avenue she asked me to return a straw hat to Saks, since she just remembered she could get the same thing at Buttner's in Hyannis for less than half the price. But I explained that hats were a nonreturnable item and stood fast in my refusal to do the errand. "Oh, all right," she said, "I'll do it myself." So she gathered up her purse and sauntered back into Saks. A few minutes later, she returned empty-handed. "They didn't want to do it," she said triumphantly, "but I talked them into it."

Many of Mrs. Kennedy's economies were amusing. For example, she always had me get old desk calendars on sale at the end of the year when they cost next to nothing. She would use them for making notes and then refer to the current calendar hanging on the wall (which was given to her every year by the church) to confirm the actual date. She never tipped bellboys, porters, taxi drivers, or hotel maids. Instead, she carried with her a supply of specially printed cards, about the size of a postcard, that had a picture of President Kennedy on the front and some of his favorite passages of Scripture on the back, along with the famous line from his inaugural address, "Ask not what your country can do for you; ask what you can do for your country." She autographed these cards and handed them out in lieu of tips, saying blithely, "Save this, someday it will be worth money."

I tried to handle her requests to economize tactfully, but sometimes the two of us ended up in a fight. This happened annually about the telephones in the Palm Beach house. Every fall when I arrived, I had the phones in the house turned on. Then Mrs. Kennedy would arrive and tell me to have them all—except hers and mine—disconnected until the guests began to arrive for the holidays. Every year I explained to her that it actually cost more to have them turned off and then back on again than it did just to leave them alone. But every year she was convinced her method of economy was more effective.

Our funniest argument was probably about the security guard. At one point she decided (wisely, I thought) that we needed a security guard on the premises. So we hired one from an agency, and they explained that we could get one without a uniform or, for an extra daily fee, a man in full uniform. After a lot of thought, Mrs. Kennedy concluded that she wanted the deterrent effect of the uniform, and so we agreed to pay the extra fee. But once the guard reported for duty, it fretted Mrs. Kennedy that he did nothing but watch, which seemed to her very much like idleness. So she came up with the idea that she could get more for her money by asking the guard to do some painting around the house while he was keeping an eye out for intruders. The guard was not particularly enthusiastic about the idea, but he finally agreed—on one condition. He wouldn't do it while he was wearing his uniform because it was expensive and he was likely to splash paint on it. I pointed out to Mrs. Kennedy that we were paying extra for the uniform and that it seemed silly to ask the guard to take it off. If we wanted a painter, we could just hire one—at a much lower hourly wage. She seemed to agree with me at that time, but later she went out and told the guard to start painting. I saw that it was useless to continue discussing the matter.

Mrs. Kennedy also found time to worry about the way other people in the family spent their money. When her grandson Christopher Lawford thoughtfully called her from school at Harvard, she reprimanded him, like a typical grandmother. "Next time, call at night because it's cheaper." When Ethel sent everyone her funny Valentine that showed her sitting on Rosie Grier's lap (he was dressed in a red costume with a silly-looking hat), Mrs. Kennedy went to the trouble of sending Ethel a hand-written note about how silly it was to waste Kennedy money mailing things like that around. When the children got together to give her a new Jacuzzi for the pool after her old one broke down, she refused to accept it on the grounds that it was too expensive. The Whirlpool dealer wouldn't take it back, so it ended up in the Smiths' summer house; Mrs. Kennedy, of course, thought it had been returned.

While Mrs. Kennedy so habitually denied herself things, she could be on the other hand a very generous gift-giver. Her friends received lovely Christmas presents: orchid plants or a bottle of Joy perfume. And she was always very sweet about remembering me at Christmas and on birthdays. The first year I was with her, she walked into the maids' dining room one afternoon when Mam'selle, Dennis, and Jim were observing my birthday with a little cake and a few gifts. Minutes later, she buzzed for me to come to her bedroom. "How much does a bottle of champagne cost?" she asked curiously. "I'd like to give you one for your birthday." And it didn't have to be a special occasion for her to do some nice little thing for me. She found out that I used the same Elizabeth Arden moisturizer that she bought in large bottles, so she told me to bring my little bottle to work with me and she would refill it from her big one. And when she realized how tiring it could be to make the long drive back and forth from the Cape to Florida (the only way to get my car back and forth), she arranged to have me take the autotrain.

But sometimes Mrs. Kennedy's sense of thrift led her to offer things that were just plain inappropriate. She meant well, but I could only smile when she gave me an old nail pencil that had obviously been used many times. It was also difficult to find the right response when she gave me a bag of her old cotton balls that she thought I might be able to get one more use out of. Perhaps the most questionable of all these gifts was one of her old worn-out bras, after she discovered that we wore the same size.

In some ways, Mrs. Kennedy just never adjusted to the idea that she was wealthy. When she first married Joe Kennedy, they lived like many other struggling young couples, watching their budget as their family grew rapidly. Despite her money and worldly position, she could often behave like any ordinary housewife. Sometimes, on the cook's day off, I would walk out to the kitchen and find Mrs. Kennedy there, in an old calico apron, merrily stirring something in a little pan that she was fixing for her lunch. (It used to worry me because her eyesight was so bad, and she would lean right over the flame in her pink nylon robe that could catch fire in a second.) You would never guess you were seeing the glamorous Rose Kennedy if you caught her in the middle of her homemaking activities. Those close to her were used to such behavior, but it sometimes surprised people who didn't know her well. For example, in 1976, she went to visit Jackie's mother, Janet Auchincloss, at Hammersmith Farms, a lovely Newport estate right on the water that afforded a wonderful view of the tall ships sailing by in that bicentennial year. When she came home, she told me that she got up in the middle of the night and went downstairs to the kitchen to fix herself a little snack. I always wondered what the staff thought when they came to work in the morning and saw her pots carefully soaking in the sink. Mrs. Kennedy had not grown up with servants and still didn't expect to have them do everything she was used to doing for herself.

Perhaps part of Mrs. Kennedy's uneasy accommodation to the family's great wealth was due to her knowledge that many people considered the Kennedy family to be nothing more than nouveau riche. That accusation had been hurled against Joe Kennedy by blue-blooded Bostonians from the moment he made his first million. Throughout the rest of his life, he retained an edge of bitterness over the snubs and exclusions the family had borne. Rose had certainly come in for her share, and they may have affected her even more deeply. Her husband at least had the satisfaction of knowing that he was outwitting most of the world, including his patrician critics, as he amassed one of the largest fortunes in the country. But Rose Kennedy had no such sense of achievement to fall back on as a consolation (except for her determination to be the mother of great men). Besides, people are usually cattier about the social failings of a wife than a husband. Women are expected to know the social proprieties and are frequently criticized when they fail to understand them. For example, I read in one of Stephen Birmingham's books that acquaintances had criticized Rose Kennedy for going out to a weekend on Long Island in a chauffeur-driven limousine, rather than driving herself in a station wagon (a real "woody" would be best) as was the accepted upper-class custom. That limo gave away that fact that she was new to monied society.

By the time I knew Mrs. Kennedy, she had had decades to learn how to blend in. She was always very observant of details such as how a table was set, how a letter was addressed, how a thank-you note was phrased, and she was careful to do all of these things "the right way" once she had learned what it was. I learned that much of her knowledge of the correct way to do things dated back to the period when she was the wife of the American ambassador to England and had a staff to explain to her all the fine points of protocol.

How she loved to remember those days! Scattered throughout both her houses were framed portraits of herself taken during that period, usually wearing a dress with a long train and a jeweled coronet in her hair. One day we were both looking at one of these photographs hanging on the sun-room wall and I said, "You were so beautiful then, Mrs. Kennedy," and she answered soberly, "Yes, yes, I was, wasn't I?" She often reminisced about the people she had met in those years in England, with special emphasis on her conversations with the King and Queen. On one visit to Windsor, she and the Queen had a good chat about the problems presented by their children. She told me that the Queen said she never had any trouble with Elizabeth (the present Queen), who was always obedient, but that her younger sister, Margaret, could be very willful and sometimes created discipline problems.

But I don't think Mrs. Kennedy was ever truly comfortable in such exalted circumstances. She was afraid she wouldn't be accepted, and I believe that fear lingered on and kept her from trying to become a part of society in Palm Beach, or Washington, or New York. She preferred to live quietly by herself, seeing few people other than family, and at least part of the reason was that such a life protected her from even having to be aware of the social barriers between herself and the old-money upper class.

I was interested to notice how many of her real friends were also women who had through marriage reached a position higher than the one they were born into. Mary Sanford, for example, was simply a Hollywood starlet before she married Laddie and eventually became one of society's *grande dames*. The Duchess of Windsor, of course, was the most famous Cinderella story of this century. C. Z. Guest had been a chorus girl before she married socially prominent Winston Guest. These were the women who put Mrs. Kennedy at her ease.

It was an ease that was difficult for her to achieve with women whose upper-class social position went back for generations. I think this was why she was always a bit in awe of her daughter-in-law, the former Jacqueline Bouvier.

It always seemed such a pity that Mrs. Kennedy could not let herself spend the money that could make her truly comfortable. The biggest problem was always the household staff, which was always too small. Her cook was also the cleaning lady, often able to do neither job well. Her chauffeur was also the gardener, or worked elsewhere during the day, with the result that she had to ask me, or one of her children, or anyone who happened to be around, to drive her where she wanted to go. One day in Hyannis Port, decorator Bob Luddington came in the back way, escorting Mrs. Kennedy. Later I asked him where they had been. "She got me to take her to church," he said in mild surprise, "and I'm not even Catholic!"

Because Mrs. Kennedy asked her household staff to do so many different jobs at one time, she was really very badly served. It was not the fault of the employees in question, who had such taxing jobs that they had to refuse to take on extra work, such as cooking for guests. As it was they would often be unable to keep up with the demands of the household when guests were in residence.

It always appalled me that so much of Mrs. Kennedy's existence was dictated by what the staff would or wouldn't do.

Family visits turned into an emotional strain; in fact, guests of any sort created a big flurry—remember what happened when Gloria Guinness merely came to tea. This made Mrs. Kennedy even more socially isolated. It kept her from inviting friends and family for meals or visits. Unquestionably, it limited the possibilities of her life. The sad thing was that all it would have taken was a few thousand more dollars a year to provide enough competent staff. It was ridiculous that the entire burden of cooking, cleaning, and serving in two large houses should fall on the shoulders of three elderly women: Mam'selle, Nellie, and Jeannette, and Nellie had kidney trouble that now requires twice-a-week dialysis. Yet she is *still* holding down the fort for the Kennedy family, baking Ted's favorite chocolate roll and her bourbon-laced cheese balls.

Poor Mrs. Kennedy. All that money and she still couldn't live comfortably.

8
Public Life

Not long after I started working for Mrs. Kennedy, she advised me to start keeping a diary of my activities as her secretary. "It will be nice for your children and grandchildren to read about your days here," she urged. "You should take advantage of these things while you have the chance. You will probably never have another job like this one," she added with a wry laugh.

As her comment indicated, Mrs. Kennedy had a very strong sense of history, and she knew her family had a secure place in the historical record of the United States. Much of her time and energy was spent in keeping the image bright. When I worked for her in the 1970s, Mrs. Kennedy was still very much in demand for personal appearances, interviews, and photographs. She was the member of the family who most seemed to symbolize its virtues for an admiring public. Old scandals might crop up to embarrass the Kennedy men, but Rose Kennedy's fame remained untarnished.

Ten years after JFK's assassination, Mrs. Kennedy continued to receive a heavy volume of mail. Strangers wrote letters of sympathy and affection. They asked for favors or jobs or financial aid. People who didn't know her personally would send flowers or handmade gifts, such as afghans, doilies, and hankies embroidered with a rose. They would send their own treasured mementos, snapshots, and beautiful cards that Mrs. Kennedy sometimes pasted up on her desk. Sometimes a letter would be prompted by a dream or a psychic vision, giving the writer an important message about the past or future to deliver to Mrs. Kennedy. Occasionally, the letters were desperate, such as the one from a man in New Delhi who said he would drink poison if he didn't receive $3,000 from Mrs. Kennedy by a certain date. (The date had already passed by the time we received the letter.) There was very little hate mail, and when such a letter did come, it was sure to be unsigned and minus any return address. Sending a hate letter to Mrs. Kennedy must have seemed as shameful as spitting on the flag.

I worked out ways of handling most of this mail without bothering Mrs. Kennedy. The volume of little gifts that came in made it impossible to accept them, so I refused all packages at the post office unless I recognized the return address. That was much simpler than taking them home, opening them up, and then repacking them to return to the sender. One time when I was away from Hyannis Port for several weeks on my own vacation, Arthur made the mistake of accepting all the packages that arrived. When I returned, I found a huge pile. Dreading the work of sending all those gifts back, I came up with the bright idea of calling Dave Powers at the Kennedy Library in Boston. That kind man was not only willing to take them off my hands, he even sent a truck to collect them. They are no doubt still neatly stored in one of the several warehouses around the Boston area that contain material the library has no room to display.

For the most part, answering the mail was a time-consuming but not difficult task. I had the engraved cards devised by a former secretary that thanked people for their letters and explained that Mrs. Kennedy was unable to answer personally. I also sent out some of the cards that Mrs. Kennedy used for tips, the ones with President Kennedy's picture on the front and some verses from the Bible on the back. Mrs. Kennedy's failing eyesight and arthritic wrists made it difficult for her to autograph these cards herself, so she asked me to learn to imitate her signature and do it for her. I sent these out in response to particularly sweet or touching letters. Another of our printed responses was a card that gave Mrs. Kennedy's recipe for Boston cream pie. It was mentioned in her book as her family's favorite dessert, and for some reason, that detail was widely publicized, so we had hundreds of requests for the recipe.

The mail also brought in many requests for interviews and appearances, especially at charity events, and Mrs. Kennedy and I had worked out some form letters to cover these situations. Usually such letters of refusal went out over my signature and said something like, "Mrs. Kennedy asks me to thank you for your letter. It has been the policy of Mr. and Mrs. Kennedy not to accept such invitations except for charities with which the family is connected. I hope you understand why she cannot make an exception in this case." I was amazed at the number of such requests.

Interestingly, the volume of mail did drop off not long after I began to work for Mrs. Kennedy. It happened about the time that reports of Judith Exner's alleged affair with Jack Kennedy in the White House hit the news media, and I suppose the drop represented some degree of disillusionment with the Kennedys. Since I didn't show Mrs. Kennedy most of the mail anyway, she had no knowledge of the change. But she did get on to the Judith Exner story, despite my efforts to keep it from her. She read about it one day in the shiny sheet, which ran a picture on the front page to accompany the story. Later that morning, Mrs. Kennedy said casually, "I saw the Exner woman's picture on the front page this morning with her large breasts. I just don't see how all that could have been going on in the White House with all the staff and other people around."

Mrs. Kennedy always handled a few pieces of mail herself, dictating replies for nearly an hour to the two or three pieces I showed her. Usually she would get tired and cross before she finished and tell me to handle the rest. She wrote regularly to a few old friends and of course to members of the family. She also corresponded with the Duchess of Windsor and sent her packages of Wrinkies, skin-colored tapes Mrs. Kennedy wore on her face to prevent wrinkles. (I think the duchess preferred the more effective remedy of plastic surgery.) The last time Mrs. Kennedy saw the Duchess in Paris, she couldn't stop talking about how old she looked. She tried to imitate the way the Duchess tottered around and nearly fell over herself. The Duchess, by the way, was ten years younger than Mrs. Kennedy.

Mrs. Kennedy was steadfast in her refusal to become involved in anything that might seem political. She was upset when Boston College announced they had named her Catholic Woman of the Year, because she never accepted such honors. She was also upset when Jackie wrote and asked her to come out in favor of the ERA. Mrs. Kennedy wrote her daughter-in-law immediately, saying she did not want to become involved in such an issue, adding that "Grandpa and I decided years ago it would be best this way."

The media often wrote or called to ask Mrs. Kennedy for interviews. A woman who was writing an article about Eunice wanted an interview to discuss her childhood. A Dutch magazine wanted to take pictures (they snapped the two of us emerging from our daily swim in the ocean). One of the networks wanted to do a program with Mrs. Kennedy and Lillian Carter (or as Mrs. Kennedy called her when she reported the offer, "Old Lady Carter"). I'm sorry that event never came off.

Mrs. Kennedy told me to refuse most of these requests, but sometimes that refusal didn't stick. I remember a big flap in the summer of 1975, when Frank Falacci of the *Cape Cod News* called to ask for a birthday interview with Mrs. Kennedy. I refused, as per policy, but afterward I mentioned it to Mrs. Kennedy because I thought it would boost her morale to know she was still in demand. "No, no," she said, "you were right, I don't want to do it." But after I left the house, she called Frank herself. During their conversation, she let slip that her son was going to run for President in 1976—the story made the front page of the *Boston Herald*.

Mrs. Kennedy also turned down most invitations. But when she did decide to attend a function, she took her duties as an ambassador for the Kennedy family very seriously. Most of her attention went into carefully planning her appearance. Even in her eighties, she was interested in fashion and proud of her looks. I always admired the spirit that kept her looking like a fashion plate at her age.

Over the years, Mrs. Kennedy had adopted certain principles to guide her in choosing her outfits. She loved hats and liked to wear large ones even though she was a small woman; she said it was all right as long as the brim didn't extend past her shoulders. She thought women should always wear something white near the face, to set off their complexions. It might be a scarf, or a piece of lace, or simply some pearls. She also thought older women ought to be sure to put something soft around the neck, to camouflage the signs of age. She favored ruffled collars or collars trimmed with lace. She tried to buy her suits and coats in neutral colors, such as black and white, on the grounds that they never went out of style and could be worn frequently witout reminding people that they had just seen that outfit. But she loved cheerful colors and had a particular weakness for vibrant shades of pink. Somehow she often ended up purchasing something in the bright shades that made her feel "up" rather than the neutral shades she considered more practical.

Mrs. Kennedy had some truly beautiful clothes to wear to formal functions. One of my favorites was a black evening gown she bought in Paris in 1975, with a velvet bodice embroidered in gold and covered with a filmy chiffon overblouse. When she modeled it for me on her return, I said, "Mrs. Kennedy, you look like you're thirty-eight in that dress." She shot back quickly, "You mean twenty-eight, don't you?" That same year she also bought a lovely red dress as well as the aqua chiffon in which she was photographed by Richard Avedon. She always willingly spent whatever it cost to buy these dresses. She once told me that Mr. Kennedy could always tell the difference between designer originals and off-the-rack clothes, no matter how carefully copied; he wanted her to wear the originals and look her best. ("And," she added thoughtfully, "he was meeting a lot of beautiful women.") So she continued to follow his preferences when it came to the wardrobe she needed for her public appearances. The only time her husband asked her not to follow fashion was when "tent" dresses were in style. He complained that he had already seen her in maternity clothes for too many years.

Mrs. Kennedy had some marvelous jewelry to wear with those gowns, too. Some of it was kept in the bank and the rest in her bedroom safe. One day she took out a pair of fabulous diamond drop earrings and asked me to take them to a jeweler's on Worth Avenue to have the clips tightened. She was afraid, she said, she might lose one when she was dancing. I loved it —I just hope that when I get into my eighties, I have to worry about losing my earrings during a bout of madcap dancing.

When she got all dressed up, Mrs. Kennedy did look wonderful. She had dark hair with only a few strands of gray; she never had to dye it. She remarked once, "My mother always had black hair, too. And she lived to be ninety-three, still really not very gray." She was willing, however, to help nature when she saw the need for it. She had had her eyes lifted several times, and her neck had been done also. But I don't believe she ever had an ordinary face-lift, because I didn't see any telltale scars.

Mrs. Kennedy also loved all the artifice of cosmetics when she was making her public appearances. She wore false eyelashes, which she put on herself—shaky hands and poor vision notwithstanding. And we often talked about such important items as the best mascara to wear and the way to apply eye shadow and our belief in the advertising claims made for various skin creams. She used Elizabeth Arden skin-care products (although she urged her granddaughter Maria to invest in some of the more expensive Laszlo line). She was always very conscientious about sticking to her beauty routines, believing in good skin care, lots of water and fresh air, moderate exercise, and a weekly massage.

For years, Mrs. Kennedy had worried about her weight and dieted rigorously to stay svelte. But by this time of her life, she no longer had a tendency to gain, and in fact she even began to drink liquid Sustagen to keep her weight up. I noticed that when she wore slacks, she had become so thin they didn't even bend when she walked. Despite her short stature, she wore clothes well because of her excellent posture and her lovely long neck, which reminded me of Audrey Hepburn's. She tried to look like Audrey Hepburn in the bust also. She thought a heavy bustline was aging to a woman, and so she had a special bra arrangement made for her in Paris. A kind of flannel was stitched over the outside of a long-line bra, which hooked onto an old-fashioned corset with stays. It gave a smoother, flatter line under her designer clothes.

Mrs. Kennedy's dedication to the job of looking her best for public appearances was really nothing short of valiant. I was especially struck by this in the fall of 1977, when her health seemed to be deteriorating. She had been in New England Baptist Hospital for nearly a week, but then she seemed to get some of her strength back. So her children decided to carry on with plans for her fall visit to Washington and New York. A few days after she arrived in New York, she called me at home in the evening to say she had done something to her knee and was unable to walk. "All that walking around Hyannis Port, up hills and over bad roads, and then I go to New York and hurt my knee," she complained. "You're just not a city girl," I teased her. Yet it was only a few days later that she called again and asked me to send her a pair of gold shoes to go with a shimmering orange dress she planned to wear to a ball. With a bad stomach and an even worse knee, she was not only going to a ball, she was determined to wear the shoes that would look best with her dress, whatever their degree of discomfort! A truly amazing woman.

But not all of her appearances were that formal. Often they were daytime activities that only called for a suit and one of her trademark big hats. For example, she attended the Palm Beach area Special Olympics for the retarded and the handicapped and made a little speech to the participants and supporters. Afterward, she gave a prize to a first-place winner, a retarded boy about thirteen years old. As she handed him the award, she enveloped him in a big bear hug and invited him to sit with her during the rest of the ceremony. That was the Rose Kennedy I especially like to remember.

One of her funnier daytime appearances came one time in Florida when she was asked to speak to a workshop on retardation that was being held at the Colonnades Hotel on Singer Island. One of the other guests at this function was John D. MacArthur, the somewhat eccentric billionaire who had established the MacArthur Foundation. MacArthur was at that time just recovering from a serious stroke, and when Mrs. Kennedy was introduced to him, she took it into her head that he was one of the retarded. On the way home, I tried to set her straight, but she never did understand who he was.

Perhaps the most unexpected public appearance was her attendance at a Republican campaign breakfast starring Nancy Reagan. This was in 1976, when Nancy's husband was making what would be an unsuccessful bid for the Republican nomination and Mrs. Kennedy's son-in-law Sarge was making what would be an unsuccessful bid for the Democratic nomination. Mrs. Kennedy read about the gathering in her morning paper and asked me if I would drive her to Junior's Restaurant in the Palm Beach Mall so she could check it out. I had assumed it would just be a big milling crowd, but it turned out to be a sit-down affair that was fully covered by the media. The moment we were escorted to our seats, the reporters showed up (Nancy had not yet made her entrance) to interview Mrs. Kennedy. She explained why she had come: "I always traveled with my father when he campaigned, and he habitually made it a point to find out what the opposition was saying and what its campaign strategy seemed to be. I'm very interested in what Mrs. Reagan has to say."

Just at that moment, Nancy Reagan entered the room and came straight over to Mrs. Kennedy to shake her hand. "It's good to see you here," Nancy said graciously, showing not a trace of the surprise she must have felt. After the speech, Mrs. Kennedy wanted to leave without going through the receiving line to shake Mrs. Reagan's hand. So she took off at full speed, wandering around hallways and back doors, looking for a way to make an unobtrusive exit; I was trotting along behind her trying to catch my breath. Suddenly we went through a doorway and found ourselves emerging onto the stage *behind* Nancy Reagan, as the receiving line crept by in front. Mrs. Kennedy squared her shoulders, stepped to the head of the line, and positively exuded charm as she shook Nancy's hand one more time. As we left the room by the official exit, she said to me, "Well, what were we to do? It was the only way out."

That night as I watched the eleven o'clock news on Channel 5, the first thing I saw was a giant close-up of my face. The entire coverage of the campaign breakfast focused on the fact that Mrs. Kennedy was there, and the interview with her was played in full. I was sure Nancy Reagan must be annoyed at being so badly upstaged. Sarge and Eunice were also annoyed, it turned out, because Mrs. Kennedy had drawn attention to the campaign of a conservative Republican at the very time she was declining to make any campaign appearances on Sarge's behalf. But despite their scowling, the next morning Mrs. Kennedy was beaming in triumph.

Mrs. Kennedy's stamina could be amazing. In the spring of 1975, she was invited to sit in the President's box at the televised premiere of a Barbra Streisand movie. The event was going to benefit the retarded, a cause in which Streisand also took a personal interest, so Mrs. Kennedy agreed to attend. When word got out that she was going to be in Washington, she was also invited to a lavish dinner at the Iranian embassy, along with Pat, Jean, Eunice, and Ted.

Several weeks before she was to leave for Washington, Mrs. Kennedy began having terrible headaches that virtually knocked her out. To cope with the pain, she relied heavily on sleeping pills, and the combination of the pain and the pills brought on another bout of stomach trouble. Her condition worried everyone. Most visits from the family were canceled and the few who did come brought their own domestics and did their best to avoid disturbing Mrs. Kennedy.

I thought it might be the better part of wisdom to cancel

the visit to Washington, but Mrs. Kennedy was determined to go. We packed a beautiful Christian Dior gown for the premiere, and a few other Paris creations for the rest of the visit, and off she went. The next evening, I watched the televised coverage, and she looked absolutely radiant. It seemed hard to believe that the stylish self-possessed regal woman I saw on television was the same person who had been unable to leave her room for days before her trip. Her ability to summon hidden reserves of energy always amazed me.

An appearance that did not go so well was the ground-breaking ceremony for the Kennedy Library. Mrs. Kennedy had just been through a serious bout of her stomach trouble and seemed both physically and mentally weak when she got in the car with Joe Gargan to drive to the ceremony. She was in a bad state when she arrived and had to be taken to the bathroom immediately; since there was a long line in front of the ladies' room, they took her into the men's. When it came time for her to take the silver-handled shovel for a ritual dig, she was so confused she didn't know which end of the shovel to use. For several days after the event, she had to stay in bed. At her age, these appearances took a lot out of her.

Yet as long as she had the strength, she tried to conceal the effects of age and illness. Many times when I drove her to some little local event in Palm Beach, such as a luncheon to benefit the retarded, she would be so weak and tired that she would lie down in the backseat during the drive. But when we arrived at our destination, she sat up, adjusted her hat, and got out of the car with her shoulders back, her chin held high, and all the poise in the world. She knew what the public expected, and as long as she was physically able, she gave it to them.

Her physical condition made it necessary for her to turn down most requests for media appearances. She said no to an idea for a bicentennial television special that would have her and her grandchildren walking the Freedom Trail in historic Boston. She turned down the invitation to appear on a talk show hosted by Kathryn and Bing Crosby. She turned down an offer of a TV special on Rosemary to help draw attention to the plight

of the retarded. She simply did not have the strength to do all the things she might have liked to do.

The one person she always said yes to was Teddy, her only remaining son. Whatever she could do to help his political career, she was willing. She would give interviews, attend receptions, make speeches. She was his secret weapon, a veteran campaigner who never failed to move audiences. Of course, that's not to say these appearances were ever easy.

I remember in particular one she made in the fall of 1976, only weeks before election day, on behalf of Ted's reelection to the Senate. His staff had arranged a reception in her honor in the ballroom of Boston's Sheraton Hotel, and sent out four thousand handwritten invitations. Mrs. Kennedy spent the morning dressing and doing her makeup, and she was looking her best when we left Hyannis Port at noon. But when we got into the suite reserved for Mrs. Kennedy at the hotel, she announced that she was tired and intended to take a nap. So she took off her clothes, ran a bath, put on her pajamas, and retired for a snooze. About the time she got up again, the suite began to fill up with people. The Senator arrived with three aides, wanting to talk about the details of Mrs. Kennedy's appearance. Joan turned up, saying she wanted to talk to Gramma, and her husband was watching her warily. Joan went into the bedroom with the announced intention of helping Gramma with her makeup, but Mrs. Kennedy refused all assistance. This led to a comic spectacle: Joan chasing Mrs. Kennedy around the room, makeup in hand, trying to catch her to apply it. On television later, it was obvious that Joan was wearing too much makeup, while Mrs. Kennedy was not wearing enough.

Finally it was time to go downstairs. As we rode the elevator down to the ballroom, Mrs. Kennedy suddenly asked me, "Barbara, did you clean up the cosmetics in my bathroom?" I said yes, although in truth I had not had the time; but I knew she shouldn't be upset or worried before she made her appearance. She was satisfied, but Ted, who knew perfectly well I had not told the truth, cocked a bold eyebrow as if to say, "Aha, I caught you!" Just one more "Don't tell Mrs. Kennedy" conspiracy.

There were thousands of people in the ballroom waiting to meet Mrs. Kennedy, and I saw her begin to shake. She was introduced to the audience by the Senator's older son, Teddy; her grandsons Christopher Lawford and David, Joe and Patrick Kennedy were also on the stage with her, as were Ted and Joan. Although she mixed up the order of her speech, it went over very well. This was the time that she told the audience how glad she was she had had that ninth child: "If I hadn't had the ninth, I would now have no sons." Some members of the audience were openly weeping, and afterward, they all wanted to crowd up on stage and shake her hand.

I saw that she was completely worn out, so I went up beside her and asked if she would like to leave. Although Ted was pressing her to stay, we went back to her room, where she changed into ordinary street clothes and wrapped a scarf around her head. Seeing her slip out the door of the hotel afterward, you would never guess that this woman had just held an audience of thousands in the palm of her hand. When we got into the car, she lay down in the backseat and closed her eyes. "It's not like it used to be," she mused, "when candidates handed out cigars with dollar bills wrapped around them at the polls on election day." Then she said to me, "You see, Barbara, if we campaign, this is what we will do. Except we'll go from town to town." I didn't reply. I knew her son hoped she would be able to do that, but it seemed out of the question at her age. Indeed, the next day, she had to be admitted to New England Baptist Hospital, for painful stomach cramps and severe diarrhea.

Another part of Mrs. Kennedy's public life was her career as a writer. Her book, *Times to Remember*, had come out in hardcover just about the time I began working for her, and she spent a lot of time autographing copies and sending them to people as disparate as Bishop Fulton J. Sheen and Al Smith's son. She had written the book with the aid of diaries she had kept for years, which I was able to take a look at. They were wonderfully detailed, telling where she went, who was there, what they said, starting from the time Joe Kennedy was appointed ambassador to England and Rose began her real public life; they also contained little swatches of the fabric of her evening gowns as well as engraved invitations and dance cards.

Her publishers, Doubleday, aware of this wealth of material, had suggested that she might like to write another book. She was tempted, I know; she refused some requests for interviews with the comment that she planned to write another book herself and didn't want to give away her material. But the truth of the matter was that she really didn't have the strength any longer for the sustained work of writing another book.

Still, she loved being an author. In an amusingly jaunty letter to Caroline, written in the winter of 1975 (about the time the paperback edition of her book came out), she talked about having more books to autograph all the time and concluded that she didn't know how many "mills" she had made but couldn't spend it anyway because it is all for the retarded children.

That was the cause that still had her total commitment. It was her own family tragedy that drew her to work on behalf of the retarded, but it was genuine personal involvement that kept her at it as her health began to fail and her vitality to run low. She made public appearances whenever she could to speak about the problem. She even did a TV spot to promote the Special Olympics in Palm Beach County. That turned into a circus. At the very last minute, Mrs. Kennedy decided to change all our thorough plans, with the result that the media people came at different times, tramped in and out through the kitchen, and parked in front of the garage instead of in the parking lot. While Mrs. Kennedy was being made up, she thought she had lost the diamond clip (shaped like a little safety pin) that she used to adjust the length of her pearls, and she went into a tizzy and got everyone else upset. (The shortener was found elsewhere, of course.) The confusion caused the makeup girl to make a mistake: Mrs. Kennedy's makeup looked much too harsh on the screen. After the taping, chaos continued to prevail as Mrs. Kennedy, on the spur of the moment, invited everyone to stay for a drink. Nellie and I had our hands full, since she wanted to serve not merely drinks but also sandwiches and coffee. In Mrs. Kennedy's hands, the simple business of taping a short public affairs spot turned into a day-long problem for all concerned. Still, except for the makeup, the finished announcement looked very good.

On another occasion, the *Ladies' Home Journal* shrewdly offered Mrs. Kennedy a contribution of $10,000 for the retarded if she would write an article about the way Christmas was celebrated in the Kennedy family. She decided that she couldn't write the article herself, but she really wanted the retarded to get that check. So she had a little talk with her son, Teddy, who then "volunteered" to write the article himself . . . for the same fee, of course. Once she talked him into taking on the job, she began to supervise him mercilessly, constantly asking him about his progress and demanding to see a draft so she could make corrections. When the article was finally finished, the magazine sent a photographer to take a picture of the author and his mother that would be run with the article. This was in Hyannis Port, and they decided to take the pictures at the point where the front lawn turns into a beach. When she was dressing, Mrs. Kennedy wanted to wear one of her Paris couturier suits and a hat, but I suggested that it seemed unsuitably formal for a family picture on the beach. So she changed to a wonderful bright red sweater and a pair of white pants, and she looked absolutely perfect. Every one of those pictures turned out well, and the one that was eventually printed made her look twenty years younger, and quite beautiful. And, of course, the best reward came later, when Teddy handed over the check he had earned for the retarded.

Mrs. Kennedy knew from firsthand experience just how expensive the care and training of a retarded child could be, so she knew that more money was always needed. She also worried about the plight of the older retarded, like Rosemary. What happened to those whose parents had died, leaving no one to take care of them anymore and no financial resources to provide substitute care? She knew of one home for older retarded people through her friends, the Morton Downeys, who had a retarded daughter there. She began to think of establishing another, and to that end she wanted to make some changes in her will, so that she could leave money for that purpose. In all Mrs. Kennedy's activities for the retarded, Eunice was her faithful lieutenant. She, too, was committed to the cause of the retarded, and she helped her mother grapple with the practical aspects of providing help.

If Eunice handled the practical side, it was Mrs. Kennedy who felt the emotional side of the problem. One day she and I were talking about the number of celebrities who were willing to work for the retarded because someone in their own family was afflicted. Mrs. Kennedy said sadly, "That's what I mean. You can have all these worldly things, but still, something like that can happen to you."

With her activities for the retarded and her position as matriarch of the Kennedy clan, Rose Kennedy was constantly in the public eye. In fact, I don't believe she ever really had a private life outside the four walls of her bedroom. Even in her own home, the curious followed her. In both Palm Beach and Hyannis Port, we more than once had the nasty surprise of finding strangers in the house, who had just walked boldly in. Sometimes the intention was simply to get a close-up glimpse of Mrs. Kennedy; sometimes I feared the possibility of darker ideas. One summer in Hyannis Port, there was a death threat against her that the FBI took seriously. Mrs. Kennedy was never told about it, but I was asked to get her out of the house so they could check it. They instructed me to whisk her off to church, where agents could keep an eye on her. She was willing to attend an afternoon mass, but somewhat perplexed by my insistence on the matter because she knew I wasn't Catholic. "Oh, well," I said, "we're all trying to get to the same place." She answered thoughtfully, "Yes, yes, you're right," but still seemed a bit puzzled. Eventually an agent who was lurking around the church told me it was all right to take her home again. Apparently, they had established that the threat was not serious.

Most people were content to stare from a distance, but even so, they were always *there*. If Mrs. Kennedy went for a walk on the beach, someone in a boat would begin to gawk. If she went into town to shop, tourists would nudge one another as she

155

passed. I guessed that one reason she went back to Palm Beach year after year was that the town took Mrs. Kennedy in its stride. There were so many rich and frequently photographed faces in Palm Beach that nobody made a big fuss over the appearance of Mrs. Kennedy.

Of course, in Hyannis Port there were always summer tourists standing at the end of the street trying to peer down and sight a Kennedy. And there was always some entrepreneur ready to take advantage of the desire to Kennedy-watch. One year I noticed a truck coming into the compound several times a week. Arthur told me it was the dry cleaner picking up and delivering at Ethel's house. But I couldn't understand why, after backing out of Ethel's drive, the truck proceeded on down to the circular driveway in front of Mrs. Kennedy's house and sometimes even went around to the parking lot in the rear. Then one day I noticed that there were people in the rear of the truck. I spoke to the guard at the end of the street about this, and he found out that the delivery man was taking people into the compound in his truck and charging them for a tour.

Being so highly visible, Mrs. Kennedy couldn't even make mistakes in private; they soon became public knowledge. I remember one time when I met Mrs. Kennedy at the airport after one of her little jaunts to Washington. The whole thing started out in a funny way, when I found Mrs. Kennedy trying to walk down the up escalator, crossly pushing the rising stairs with her foot as if to say, "You *will* go down." When we finally emerged, we got into the Lincoln, which I had parked near the exit door. But when I tried to put my key in the ignition, it wouldn't fit. Puzzled, I tried again several times. Then I noticed a pair of leather gloves on the front seat, which were certainly not mine. I looked in the rearview mirror and saw an identical Lincoln— same model, same year, same color—parked behind us. It dawned on me that we were in someone else's car! As we got out, I noticed the guard grinning. He came over and told me he had noticed the second car pull up in front of me and had feared there would be a mix-up. The point of the story is that the anecdote was all over the airport before nightfall. When Ted came in the next day to stay with his mother, several people told him about it immediately. He thought it was a great story and teased us about it for days. But it made me realize that a public figure has to expect that even little gaffes like that will become public knowledge.

I'm sure that her constant celebrity was in some ways a trial to Mrs. Kennedy. And yet she obviously enjoyed being in the limelight. When she encountered tourists looking for her after mass, she would walk right up to them and say, "Hello, I'm the President's mother. That's his pew right over there." She loved to have her picture taken with any member of the family, at any time of day, by either professional or amateur photographers. She always studied published photographs carefully to see how she looked, and would decide accordingly to wear more or less makeup, adjust the angle of her hat, retire one outfit or wear another more frequently. She didn't like it when pictures made her look old, though. There is a famous photo of the Kennedy family taken in 1960, the morning after election day, when the close race was finally called and all the world knew John F. Kennedy would be the next president. The photographer in charge had arranged it so that Mrs. Kennedy was seated next to Jackie, whose youthful glow does indeed make Mrs. Kennedy look like the "older generation." That particular photo was nowhere to be seen in either of Mrs. Kennedy's houses.

Mrs. Kennedy always seemed very conscious of her place in history. She once remarked, as we were peacefully swimming in the ocean, "Mr. Kennedy was so lucky to have me for a wife. I had gone to college and was well educated, whereas the other girls from East Boston were just high school graduates. I had traveled abroad, met Sir Thomas Lipton, spoke French and German." What she meant was that she was prepared to play a part in the Kennedy dynastic history. As daughter of a mayor, wife of an ambassador, mother of a president and two senators, she knew she would be read about by generations to come.

Naturally she always took a great interest in books, magazine articles, and television shows about the Kennedy family. One of my first tasks when I started to work for her was to go through her copy of *The Founding Father*, a biography of Joe Kennedy, and transcribe the comments she had made in the margins about what she felt were inaccuracies. She wrote to an old friend in England to tell her not to be tempted to read Lord Longford's book on the Kennedys because he had called Joe Kennedy "predatory towards women." She watched the tape of the TV special called *Rose Kennedy: Good Times, Bad Times* without any comment . . . and then watched it again. Together, she and I watched a special Mike Douglas show that focused on her book, with a long personal interview and film clips and photographs as well. I found it rather odd to see on the flickering screen those photographs that now seemed so familiar in their spots on the wall or in their silver frames on top of a table. Mrs. Kennedy kept up a running commentary. She worried about the way her makeup looked in the interview. She wondered aloud why they didn't mention the fact that proceeds from the book were going to help the retarded. When they showed pictures of the inauguration, she remembered how cold Jack had been with no coat, and how Jackie was also freezing because there had been no time for the tailor to put a lining in her coat. "They put the parents at the end of the podium where we couldn't really see what was happening," she remarked crossly.

When the show was over, there was a long silence. Then she said slowly, "How could that happen? Two boys in one family assassinated. . . ." To break the growing feeling of sorrow, I said quickly, "Mrs. Kennedy, I thought the program was done very well. And you looked fantastic in your interview." She answered, "Of course, dear, it's only natural you feel that way, since you are here now and know the family." Then she walked to her bed to straighten out the spread and I went to help her. It was a gesture we were to repeat many times in years to come, a silent signal that an emotional moment was over and done with.

Another program she watched with interest was *Young Joe Kennedy, the Forgotten Prince*. I mentioned having seen the previews, which appeared to contain some love scenes. She commented, "I don't remember him being in love with anyone in particular. It was always Jack who had some girl. He was so

much in love with the Finklestein girl up the street. She married a boy she fell in love with in high school. She was very unsophisticated and rather tomboyish, but Jack was wild about her."

But it was not just the Kennedy family that she found fascinating to follow in the media. I remember with amusement when she watched *Eleanor and Franklin* on television. Her chief comment? "Sarah Roosevelt [FDR's mother] died when she was eighty-seven, didn't she?" When she read a report that Amy Carter had sat down at the piano after some White House dinner, she exclaimed, "How absurd! To get all dressed up and attend a dinner party and afterwards have to sit and listen to some nine-year-old play the piano." When she read about how the Fords entertained Queen Elizabeth and Prince Philip, she criticized their choice of a menu. They had served a veal roast, which she pointed out was not particularly American. "When I gave a dinner for the King and Queen at the embassy," she recalled, "I thought it should be a regular American dinner with corn on the cob, turkey, sweet potatoes, ice cream, and strawberry shortcake."

When Rose Kennedy thought history was in danger of making a mistake about a member of the family, she was capable of vigorous action. For example, she was quite distressed to read in one of James Reston's columns his statement that President Kennedy was not a religious man. She fired off a letter in return, stating, "Like his brothers and sisters, my son Jack was reared in a home with a deep and abiding faith. He practiced that faith constantly until his death."

Sometimes it was her own family she had to set straight. One day at a family lunch in Hyannis Port she and Ted were talking about *Camelot*, the musical he had taken her to see the night before. She commented that people had referred to President Kennedy's administration as "Camelot" because it strove for certain ideals. Ted said he would like to get away from that label. "It implies royalty, or a dynasty," he commented, obviously understanding the political liabilities of such a connotation. In fact, he concluded, it was really the opposite with the Kennedys, who were just plain people who liked things like hominy and grits. Mrs. Kennedy looked at her son in amazement and then said spiritedly, "We do not!" The whole family laughed in acknowledgment of the truth of her protest. Not even Ted Kennedy could be allowed to rewrite what Mrs. Kennedy knew to be the truth behind the Kennedy legend.

In a broad sense, you could say that most of Mrs. Kennedy's time was spent in arranging the way the Kennedy family would go down in history. That was why she was so concerned about the disposition of all those things in the attic: They were part of a historical record. She made arrangements to give the desk on which President Kennedy signed the Nuclear Test Ban Treaty to Caroline and John, but most of the papers, photos, and memorabilia went to the Kennedy Library or the Kennedy Birthplace. She rather hoped, in fact, that the Hyannis Port house might also become a museum, open to the public: "After all," she remarked, "it's where the President spent most of his time growing up." She thought carefully over the disposition of each and every scrap of family history. One dress was donated to the Smithsonian, another to the library. These papers were put away in the bank vault, those given to the library. One day, young Christopher Kennedy was in my office and happened to see a pile of things that were being sent off to the library as per Mrs. Kennedy's instructions. "Why does Gramma give everything to the library?" he asked plaintively. "I'd like to have something that belonged to Uncle Jack."

But for Mrs. Kennedy, this was a matter that transcended personal sentiment. Her most important mission, in the years left to her, was safeguarding the memory of her husband and her sons.

9

The Grandchildren

An important part of the Kennedy legacy was the next generation. Mrs. Kennedy had twenty-nine grandchildren . . . twenty-nine chances for another president, senator, or attorney general. Yet the grandchildren also provided Mrs. Kennedy with twenty-nine reasons to worry.

Mrs. Kennedy's ideas about bringing up children had crystalized when her own were young, more than fifty years earlier. She had been a good disciplinarian, a patient developer of their abilities, a moral guide, and a continual good example. She sent her children to church regularly, she checked their homework every night, she dutifully recorded their heights and weights several times a year, she made sure they visited the dentist. She kept track of each child's shoe size, food preference, and serious illnesses; she also gave special attention to the ones who needed to be encouraged to speak up and the ones who needed a good dose of discipline. Her success as a mother was one of her proudest accomplishments, and she knew it was the reason she would go down in history.

But when Mrs. Kennedy tried to apply her old-fashioned notions to the raising of her grandchildren, they often seemed hopelessly out-of-date. For example, she sent them all a memo (formally headed from "Mrs. Joseph P. Kennedy") telling them to drink more milk to make their teeth nice and white—and she really believed this was true. Her son Jack had done it, she said, with excellent results. She sent other memos urging them to watch their grammar or to see certain programs on television that she thought would be educational. She instructed her children to subscribe to Catholic family magazines so the grandchildren would absorb their wholesome point of view.

I think she was dimly aware that her prescriptions for the Kennedy grandchildren's upbringing were hopelessly inadequate. For these were no ordinary children. They were kids who had played hide-and-go-seek in the White House, concealing themselves under the President's desk. Senators and congressmen were regular dinner guests; so were famous actresses and Pulitzer Prize winners. During the crisis surrounding the integration of the University of Alabama, top-ranking officials of the Justice Department who called the attorney general with updated reports often chatted with one of Bobby's kids before they got down to business, and young children frequently sat in their fathers' laps as world affairs were debated and decided. The grandchildren had been constantly photographed from their earliest youth and were resigned to the fact that all of their actions would be reported in the news media. And, of course, in one way or another, all of the children were victims of the violence and tragedy that had struck the Kennedy family. Small wonder that they had some problems as they were growing up.

Many of these problems were concealed from Mrs. Kennedy. She worried about the fact that they might be drinking Coke and thus harming their teeth; it never occurred to her that they might be using it. When David Kennedy was first hospitalized for his drug problem, his grandmother was told that he had a bad case of the flu that turned into pneumonia, a story she apparently accepted without question. When Christopher Lawford was later treated for the same problem, she had no more inkling of the truth of the matter. In fact, I shared much of her innocence. Although I was working there at the time and spending all day in the compound, I too had no idea of the extent or the severity of the problem. We knew nothing about it until it began to be covered in the news media. The adults in the family were skilled at covering the problem up—which had, of course, been another part of the problem.

Yet I certainly was aware that many of the grandchildren seemed spoiled and willful. When any of them were around, they frequently made my already difficult job just a little bit harder. For example, stationery, pens, and pencils steadily disappeared from my desk whenever they were around and sometimes I couldn't find paper to write a letter on. Once in Hyannis Port, Bobby Shriver was bold enough to take the typewriter right off my desk, carrying it home to his house where he was working on an overdue paper for school. I was unable to handle any of Mrs. Kennedy's correspondence until he was persuaded to return it. (Mrs. Kennedy wrote him a letter telling him in the future he should rent a typewriter when he needed one.) I was advised by the maids and former secretaries alike that I should keep the petty cash locked up or the grandchildren would take it as well. Many of them had the habit of borrowing small sums—five or ten dollars—from a maid or chauffeur and never paying it back.

One issue that caused continual trouble the whole time I worked there was the use of Mrs. Kennedy's car. With the number of teenage kids in the family, there were never enough cars around for them all. In Palm Beach, where everyone flew down to visit, the shortage could be especially acute. The grandchildren all loved to borrow their grandmother's Lincoln Continental, but they were usually irresponsible about caring for it or returning it. Several of them borrowed it for a day in Hyannis Port when it was practically brand-new and returned it covered with scratches from driving it through the heavily wooded acres of undeveloped land Joe Kennedy had bought some years before near Osterville. Bobby Shriver borrowed it once for the afternoon and took off with a bunch of friends (five in all) and a German shepherd; I winced to think of the effect on the upholstery. Then it turned out that he wanted to keep the car for two weeks and use it to go back to Yale. Since Mrs. Kennedy was in Europe at the time, I felt I couldn't take the responsibility for making that decision. Once the car got as far away as New Haven, who knew if I would ever get it back in time to go to Palm Beach? As I hesitated, Bobby told me firmly that I had nothing to worry about. "I called Mummy and she said I could. And after all, Mummy is her *daughter*," he added, making it plain that the status of a secretary was vastly inferior. I made several calls to both Sarge and Eunice about the matter, but neither of them really wanted to take the responsibility for telling me to give Bobby the Lincoln. In the end, Sarge decided that Bobby should rent a car to take back to school. Since Bobby had already spent his allowance for the next two months, he couldn't pay for the car himself, and he didn't have a valid credit card. So I drove him to the car rental place at the Hyannis airport and used my own card, sending the slip on to the New York office for reimbursement. Some weeks later, they called back to inquire why I had rented a car for Ethel's son Joe. It turned out that Bobby had playfully signed Joe's name to the bill so his cousin's account would be charged instead of his own.

That winter I had a rerun of the same argument with Bobby's sister, Maria. She was staying in Palm Beach for a few days while her grandmother was away, and she wanted to take Mrs. Kennedy's car to drive to a party in Miami. This time I was sure the answer should be no, especially since Mrs. Kennedy had recently been having trouble with the car and wanted me to take it to a garage to be fixed. But Maria didn't like to take no for an answer, and she, too, assured me that her mother had said it was perfectly all right. I called Eunice to discuss the situation, and Maria was very angry when she found out. "You shouldn't have bothered Mummy. She has enough on her mind right now." (This was the year that Sarge was making a run for the presidency.) Eunice suggested that we should settle the problem as we had done before, by renting Maria a car. But before I could get that done, Eunice called back to say that on second thought she didn't want her daughter to go to that party in Miami anyway.

Eventually, it was decided in a family council that none of the grandchildren would be allowed to borrow Mrs. Kennedy's car again. If they genuinely needed one, I would get them a rental. One of the first victims of this new policy was Christopher Lawford, visiting his grandmother in Palm Beach. Of course, he needed a car to get around and see friends, so Mrs. Kennedy told me to rent one for the duration of the trip. Always mindful of unnecessary expenses, she added that I should get an economy rental. I ended up with a Gremlin, and poor Christopher was mortified at having to drive that low-budget model around snobby Palm Beach, meeting friends who were driving expensive imports.

Occasionally I let some of the grandchildren use my own car to run errands or go to lunch nearby. Caroline was always very responsible about getting my car back at the time she promised, and appreciative of the favor. In many ways, she seemed more adult than the rest of her generation. Unlike most of them, she always made an effort to carry on a conversation when I drove her—to the airport or to the doctor for allergy shots—and I found her generally interesting to talk to.

It was Caroline who pointed out to me how much getting together for the holidays—Christmas and Easter in Palm Beach, Fourth of July and Labor Day in Hyannis Port—meant to all the grandchildren. It was their only real family continuity, she explained, in lives that were full of change and travel. Many of the grandchildren were away in boarding school for much of the year, and frequently their holidays were spent elsewhere. This peripatetic life-style made it hard for them to maintain friendships . . . as did the very fact of being a Kennedy. So the cousins looked forward to being together at those big holiday gatherings. It's what made it worth it to Caroline to sleep on a rented cot in the Palm Beach house, scrub the front door mat on her hands and knees, and confront photographers every time she tried to swim. Even today, I notice, when Jackie has more or less abandoned the compound in favor of her house on Martha's Vineyard, Caroline continues to use the Hyannis Port house whenever she can get away in the summer. It allows her to stay in touch with her Kennedy relatives, many of whom she rarely sees the rest of the year.

By the mid-1970s, the grandchildren especially treasured those holiday get-togethers because they were separated most of the time. It was about that time that Ethel and Bobby's son Joe had the accident while driving the Jeep on Nantucket that injured his brother David and left David's girlfriend paralyzed. Various of the teenage male Kennedys were buying and using drugs and getting into scrapes with the law because of it. Arthur even discovered marijuana plants growing in unsuspecting Jackie's garden! The result of all this was apparently a family council that resolved to send the older children away for the summers; the combination of the free time in Hyannis Port and the encouragement of cousins was thought to be pernicious. So every summer thereafter, the teenage grandchildren were dispersed. Some went to Indian reservations to work, others interned in congressional offices, others traveled.

So it was only on the holidays that they saw one another again. Perhaps one reason those holidays always seemed so frantic was that the kids were trying to make up for lost time together. They played tennis, went sailing or fishing, walked around the compound together. Since I saw many of them only once a year, it was sometimes difficult to tell them apart. You could always pick out Ethel's son Bobby Kennedy, though, because he would stroll around with an exotic bird on his shoulder or an unusual pet of some sort following behind.

I have to admit that my own relationship with many of the grandchildren was not very good. I was in the awkward position of having to enforce Mrs. Kennedy's commands or take responsibility for her property, so I constantly had to oppose their wishes. For example, Maria Shriver called me in Hyannis Port one day in the fall, after Mrs. Kennedy had left for Paris, and said she would like to bring some friends over one evening to see a movie. This, of course, was exactly what Mrs. Kennedy had strictly prohibited, and I had to tell Maria so. She persisted in her request, so finally I called Mrs. Kennedy's nephew Joe Gargan for advice. He agreed that I should not take the responsibility for going against Mrs. Kennedy's command, but he called his cousin Eunice to get her explicit permission, which she gave. Although Maria and her friends promised to clean up after themselves, I found trash in the theater the next morning, and all the mirrors upstairs had lipstick prints on them. Since Jeannette was never employed when Mrs. Kennedy was away from Hyannis Port, there was no one to clean up the mess except me.

Mrs. Kennedy took a special interest in Maria, who was her godchild. She wrote Maria letters recommending operas and ballets that she ought to see to improve her cultural awareness. She also advised her that by the age of twenty-one she should get into the habit of taking good care of her skin. Maria was one of the most attractive of the granddaughters, and Mrs. Kennedy always liked to see her dressed formally and looking her best. She lent Maria that fabulous triple-strand pearl necklace (which Maria will one day inherit) to wear to meet Prince Charles, and Maria did indeed look lovely on that occasion. Of course, Mrs. Kennedy also felt free to criticize Maria when she didn't live up to Kennedy expectations. An example was the summer that Maria appeared at the compound in a halter top. It was not especially revealing by present-day standards, but Mrs. Kennedy was horrified. She immediately fired off a letter to Maria's father asking him why he permitted Maria to "show her breasts" that way. In the future, whenever Maria was around the compound, she was more decorously dressed.

Mrs. Kennedy was never hesitant about expressing her disapproval of any aspect of the grandchildren's behavior. She got mad at Willie Smith because he consumed so many soft drinks, which she was sure was bad for his teeth. Christopher Lawford came in for his share of criticism because he asked for breakfast in bed when he was visiting Palm Beach; Mrs. Kennedy thought that was an unnecessary luxury that kept Nellie from attending to more important work. She was taken aback when she discovered that Ethel's children didn't tip the servants when they were visiting someone but mistakenly tipped the hostess instead, so she immediately wrote Ethel instructing her to correct their mistake. She was extremely irate when she heard that the grandchildren complained about having to use plastic glasses at the pool in Palm Beach. "I will not take that sort of gas!" she exclaimed. "They either drink out of plastic glasses or go thirsty. There is no reason to take good glasses to the swimming pool or tennis court."

Looking back at my notes, it is sad to see how many of Mrs. Kennedy's letters to her grandchildren contained complaints about their behavior or refusals of their requests. She wrote to David Kennedy to tell him he couldn't come for Easter because there wasn't enough room, and added that he might try to come later when "we could probably squeeze you in"—not exactly an open-arms welcome. David's sister Kathleen and her husband were also disinvited for the same reason. She wrote a querulous letter to Anthony Shriver telling him she thought of him as she walked on the lawn in Palm Beach, because "the holes that you people made playing ball during Christmas" were finally almost green again.

Sometimes, instead of writing directly to the grandchild, she wrote to a parent. She told the Senator that he ought to encourage Kara to speak up more at home so she would overcome her shyness and learn to take part in discussions.

Yet Mrs. Kennedy could also be a loving and supportive grandparent. When Ethel's daughter Courtney went to college at Stanford and found that she had trouble adjusting to California life and living so far away from the rest of the family, Mrs. Kennedy wrote her a warm letter, encouraging her to strive to adapt to her new surroundings and telling her that she had felt just the same when she had gone away to school in Germany. She concluded by telling Courtney to have faith in herself, faith in her program, and faith in God, and "to decide this year is going to be one of the best years of your life." She was proud of Bobby Kennedy's television special about the wild animals of Africa and impressed by the fact that he was paid several hundred thousand dollars for it. She wrote to him after another public appearance to tell him she thought his speech was excellent. (She closed by coquettishly telling him to "come down any time with a pal, preferably male!") After young Teddy lost his leg, she wrote proudly that he was a wonderful example to everyone and urged him to keep up the good work, even though she understood that it was not always easy.

She was careful to remember every grandchild's birthday, and she communicated with most of them frequently. Once she found some funny postcards at the local drugstore to send to Ethel's children, and she was crestfallen when I said I was afraid they might be stolen in the mail for the value of her signature. I suggested putting them in an envelope, but she said crossly, "What fun is that?" A few hours later, she came back with her solution to the problem: She had written the message upside down.

Of all her grandchildren, Mrs. Kennedy was perhaps closest to Caroline. She worried about the effect of the problems Caroline had already encountered in her young life, and she wrote to her granddaughter whenever she saw her name in the news. She wrote to say how sorry she was when Aristotle Onassis was ill; and when Teddy went to the Onassis funeral, his overseas call to Mrs. Kennedy was chiefly to tell her how Caroline and John were handling the crisis. She was concerned when the house where Caroline was staying in England was bombed by a terrorist group, and she was sympathetic about the problems Caroline had in being followed constantly by the press. Her letters to Caroline were both affectionate and supportive; she said that she often thought of Caroline's father and how proud he would have been of her and how delighted with her progress. She made special arrangements to be sure that Caroline and her brother, John, would get things that had belonged to their father. In her will she arranged to leave them not only the President's valuable desk but a painting that had been one of his favorites.

Mrs. Kennedy was also very concerned about Ethel's son David, although she didn't know all the details of his problems. He often looked pale and unwell, and that worried her greatly. Later she read in the papers that David had been arrested on drug charges, and, of course, that upset her, too. We discussed it when I went back to visit her in Hyannis Port in the fall of 1979. She thought it was a tragedy for Ethel's sons that their father wasn't around to guide them. She added, "Mr. Kennedy was so wonderful in that respect." Perhaps that was why she always put a lot of faith in a father's influence. I remember she used to sympathize with the problems I had in bringing up two children alone and worried about how hard it must be for me as a single parent.

Several years later Nellie gave me an account of Mrs. Kennedy's last visit with her grandson David. Actually, I saw her just a few days before he died, during that Easter vacation of 1984. It was a distressing visit, because she was very feeble and confused. Her eyes were so bad that she was sitting only a foot or two away from her huge television set, and she didn't know me until I began to talk. She was not able to feed herself, and I hated watching the nurse spoon food into her mouth. Our conversation was pitifully brief. I asked her if she was getting ready to go to the Cape; she looked at me in perplexity and asked, "Where am I now?" I told her she was in Palm Beach, and she said, "Then it must be too cold to go to the Cape." Nellie told me this was the most she had said in days; I think she instinctively associated my presence with working or answering questions.

David saw Mrs. Kennedy one or two days later, and only a day or two before he died. Apparently he and his younger brother Doug turned up at the Brazilian Court Hotel without any advance notice. Even if his grandmother had known he was coming, David couldn't possibly have stayed at the house, because it was extremely crowded. The Senator and his son Teddy were there, as were Pat Lawford, Steve and Jean Smith, and Eunice. It was so crowded that Sydney Lawford and Ted's younger son, Patrick, were sharing a room, and Sarge had decided to go stay at the Breakers, Palm Beach's exclusive hotel, rather than fight the mob scene at the house. Apparently Doug called the house several times asking for Patrick, but always missed him. Finally Doug called again to say he and David wanted to come visit their grandmother. Nellie showed them up to Mrs. Kennedy's room, and she told me David later came out crying. It had been a long time since he had seen her, and he was upset by the deterioration in her physical and mental condition.

That's an indication of what Mrs. Kennedy meant to her grandchildren . . . the indomitable matriarch was at the heart of the family unity and continuity. Yet for the sake of her own health, it was necessary to keep many of the family problems hidden from her. She was certainly unaware of the swirl of family controversy over David's situation in the late 1970s. On the advice of Steve Smith, David had been sent to a hospital in California for treatment of his drug problem. Steve was angry because David's mother refused to sign the papers taking full responsibility for this step. In the end, it was Kathleen Kennedy who put herself on the line to help her brother.

The fact that David had not seen his grandmother for several years was not particularly unusual. Although Mrs. Kennedy kept in touch with all the grandchildren by letter, she frequently seemed to discourage their actual presence. Part of the reason was the usual one that she didn't have a domestic staff that could handle guests without disruption. Her age also had something to do with it. In her eighties, she was understandably set in her ways and no longer open to many new experiences. The pleasures of the young completely mystified her. She once wrote to Caroline about the way "the younger crowd" behaved in Palm Beach, explaining that the schedule was to start out at 1:00 A.M. and wander from one nightclub to another. The result, which Mrs. Kennedy deplored, was that the grandchildren were sleeping through "the best part" of the Florida day. In another letter to "Moucher," the Dowager Duchess of Devonshire, she made the same complaint and added that she heartily disapproved of the system. "It is really awful," she said, but comforted herself with the thought that the grandchildren were there only a few weeks a year during their school vacations.

It's easy to see why the grandchildren were somewhat uncomfortable about their visits to Gramma. She kept careful track of their comings and goings and tried to inform herself of the time at which each guest came home at night. Since her bedroom was right over the front porch in both her houses, it was hard to sneak in without her knowing it. This was why all the grandchildren wanted to stay in what was called the President's Bedroom when they came to visit. In both Hyannis Port and Palm Beach, the President's Bedroom was a comfortably furnished room on the ground floor, rather than upstairs with the rest of the bedrooms, and it had a private entrance, which had been very convenient when President Kennedy was visiting his parents and trying to conduct the business of state at the same time. The grandchildren wanted to stay there not because of the historical association, but because of the freedom offered by that private entrance. Of course, Ted liked to stay in the President's Bedroom for the same reason, and you can be certain he always got first choice. But if he wasn't around, the boys all tried to get to stay there.

Occasionally, Mrs. Kennedy put a spike in their advance planning by tell Mam'selle or Jeannette to lock up the entire house at night, including the separate entrance to the President's Bedroom. In Palm Beach, this left the grandchildren with no choice but to wake someone up in order to get back home after a long night of fun. In Hyannis Port, one grandson found an alternative. Since the house there was built up off the ground, there was a short staircase to the private entrance, and he simply stood on the staircase and jimmied the lock on the nearby window, then crawled in. It was worrisome to discover how simple it was for him to break in.

Visits to Gramma had other difficult moments. Many of them came in the dining room. What with her lifelong commitment to dieting, her bad stomach, and her usual fare of plain things plainly cooked, Mrs. Kennedy had by this stage of her life virtually lost all interest in food. And it seemed that she didn't understand why others didn't feel exactly the same way. For example, at mealtimes you were supposed to discuss world affairs, not the food you were eating; there was no enthusiastic gourmet talk about the perfect little young lettuce leaves or an exquisitely ripe piece of cheese, no comparison of dressings made with walnut or extra-extra-virgin olive oil from Greece, no rhapsodizing over a light piece of pastry or an unctuously smooth sauce. Mrs. Kennedy's etiquette seemed to require that you ate with as little attention to your food as possible.

It also required that you *ate* as little food as possible. Mrs. Kennedy had settled on a rather odd form of service at her table. When the meal began, bowls and platters were served to each person, in the formal European style; it was usually Mam'selle in Palm Beach and Jeannette in Hyannis Port who performed this ceremony. But then, instead of passing the food around again a little later, they simply put all the dishes on the sideboard and left the room. So anyone who wanted a second helping had to get up from the table, walk over to the sideboard, and serve himself. I suppose, in a relaxed atmosphere, this might have encouraged some people to help themselves to a generous encore, but in Mrs. Kennedy's dining room, she was sure to be watching you intently. You could practically hear her counting the peas going onto the plate, estimating the size of a piece of meat—and looking critically at the person who proposed to eat all those calories to calculate the damage to figure or complexion. Only the hungriest and skinniest of her teenage grandsons ever dared help themselves to seconds.

The granddaughters were especially careful to watch what they ate in Mrs. Kennedy's presence, because she could be quite harsh about any tendency toward plumpness. Ted's daughter, Kara, went through a period of overweight in her early teens, and Mrs. Kennedy worried about it constantly. She felt most of her granddaughters suffered from a figure flaw anyway: She thought they tended toward heavy thighs. Whenever she pointed that out, as she did about Caroline, Maria, Kara, and the three Lawford girls, she was always quick to add that the problem came from the *Kennedy* side of the family. Once the *Star* ran a picture story that she just loved, putting forth the thesis that Rose Kennedy had a better figure than any of her granddaughters and demonstrating it through carefully selected photos. You had better believe that she clipped that article to save! I would love to know what the granddaughters thought—after all, it's not a very flattering kind of publicity.

In view of all this, it was not really surprising that the older grandchildren preferred to visit when their grandmother wasn't at home. For example, Ethel's son Joe stayed in the apartment over Mrs. Kennedy's garage one winter, working on a fishing boat and hanging out with local friends. Unfortunately, he left the place looking like a disaster area, and Mrs. Kennedy was very angry about it. Later Joe's brother Bobby, then in his early twenties, stayed alone in the Palm Beach house one summer, working on his book about Alabama judge Frank Johnson; I don't believe Mrs. Kennedy ever learned of his extended stay. I do remember discussing the issue of Bobby's book with Jean Smith, who told me she had pulled strings with friends in the New York publishing community to help get the book published. I commented on the fact that a book was nevertheless quite an achievement for a young man his age and added, "I hear Bobby is going to be good political meat for the future." Jean looked right at me, cocked an eyebrow quizzically, and said flatly, "I doubt that very much."

One reason the grandchildren preferred to use Mrs. Kennedy's homes only when she herself was absent was that they frequently brought companions of the opposite sex. I remember the time Maria Shriver came to stay for a few days in Palm Beach. I assumed she had come alone and was surprised when I walked through the dining room the next morning and found her having breakfast with a young man. On another occasion, Christopher Lawford brought a girlfriend to Palm Beach, at the same time Ted was there with a semiregular local girlfriend much younger than himself. The two "dates" became very chummy, chatting about makeup and putting on rock music and dancing together as the two Kennedys watched. It was a bizarre scene that could have come right out of a decadent Italian movie.

It seemed that where the grandchildren were concerned, it was one "Don't tell Mrs. Kennedy" situation after another. There was the discovery that Sydney Lawford, after asking her grandmother for money to put gas in the car, charged the gas on Mrs. Kennedy's account at the local station and used the money for personal spending. There was the time that a perplexed tow-truck operator called and asked what to do with

Stevie Smith's BMW, which he had left in Lynn, Massachusetts, with only the vague instruction to tow it to New York
—no address given. There was the time Christopher Lawford
left the door to the beach dressing rooms open at the Palm
Beach house and some stranger simply wandered into the
house. Whenever possible, there was a conspiracy of silence
about such events so they wouldn't upset Mrs. Kennedy.

But sometimes the grandchildren's misdeeds could not
be kept from her. She had a real instinct for uncovering things
we were trying to hide. For example, once Victoria Lawford
and Jackie's son, John, made brownies in the Hyannis Port
kitchen and then tracked the sticky chocolate batter all over
the white rug in the living room. Before anyone could clean
it up, Mrs. Kennedy arrived on the scene. She got that look
—with the cold eyes and the dilated nostrils—that was enough
to make anyone feel ashamed and embarrassed. She got that
same look when she found me in the office writing a check to
the airlines for fifteen dollars to pay for the cost of a little dog
that Victoria and Robin Lawford brought with them on the
plane. When they arrived at the airport, carrying the dog in
a satchel, they were told they would have to pay extra for the
dog. They called me (at home in the evening) in tears because
they didn't have the money. I called the airline manager (also
at home in the evening) and asked him if he would let them
on the plane with the dog if I would promise to send a check
the next morning, and he finally agreed. But Mrs. Kennedy
caught me in the act of writing the check, and the whole story
came out. She made sure that the fifteen dollars was billed to
Sydney and Robin by the New York office, and fumed about
how they ought to be old enough to learn to check into things
like that the next time.

Yet Mrs. Kennedy never let any momentary irritations
stand in the way of her efforts to teach the grandchildren the
Kennedy way of doing things. She constantly urged them all
to try to do their very best. She suggested that Kathleen should
start typing her correspondence because her handwriting was
not legible. In a memo to all the family about an episode of

Alistair Cooke's *America* dealing with Irish immigration, she reminded them that they lived in a great country: "when you think of someone coming over in 1864 with no education but a lot of guts," whose descendant became not just an eloquent speaker but also the President of the United States. She had me send copies of Longfellow's poem on the ride of Paul Revere to every Kennedy household so the grandchildren could memorize the poem and recite it at a family picnic on the Fourth of July. She also sent them facsimile copies of the Declaration of Independence and pointed out how many of the signers had attended Boston Latin School, the rigorous private academy where both Joe Kennedy and John F. Fitzgerald had been students. When it seemed that Bobby's son Joe might run for office, Mrs. Kennedy wrote his sister Kathleen an enthusiastic letter. She mentioned once again that she had always preferred being the mother of a great man to being a great woman herself, and added that it might be even more of a thrill to be the grandmother of a great man. And she seemed sincerely disappointed when Caroline obeyed Jackie's wishes and bowed out of accompanying her grandmother to a political tea. Everyone in the family knew that Jackie didn't care for the hustle of "press-the-flesh" campaigning. Mrs. Kennedy still believed politics was a noble profession and hoped to see more of her grandchildren involved in it.

When the grandchildren visited, she tried to imitate the kind of conversation that Joe had insisted on when his children were growing up. At the dinner table, she asked them various questions, such as, "What is the meaning of Passover?" or "Why does Lent last forty days?" "What is a sheik?" or "Why is the Middle East different from the Far East?" Other times, she asked questions she herself was curious about, but it sometimes developed that no one else knew the answer, either, so such discussions ended up being of little educational value. But she never stopped trying to make the grandchildren interested in world affairs and curious about the things they read or saw. One year when we were talking about what we needed to take to Palm

Beach, Mrs. Kennedy told me to go out and buy a map of Africa so everyone would be able to follow the political change there.

She liked to listen to her grandchildren talking, to get an idea of what kinds of things interested the younger generation. The pool was a great place for this kind of information-gathering. As she dog-paddled back and forth to get her daily exercise, she could hear what the grandchildren, lounging around the pool with cold drinks, were saying. One day she told me, "These children are so advanced. The other day I heard them talking about pregnancy and the fetus . . . the fetus! Why, I hardly knew what the fetus was myself until about two years ago!"

It amused me to hear her use words she had picked up from listening to the grandchildren. One was "gas," which she used when she was complaining about their refusal to drink out of plastic glasses. Another day I heard her say, "Excuse me, I have to go to the john." Startled, I exclaimed, "What?!" She answered defensively, "Well, that's what everyone else calls it nowadays." It was all part of her determined effort to keep up, like looking up new words—"trendy," for example—and copying down her expressions for dinner conversation. Her grandchildren provided Mrs. Kennedy with a window on the world of the younger generation.

Children evoked in Mrs. Kennedy a tenderness that nothing else could by this time of her life. She would always say hello to the children or grandchildren of neighbors. She responded with great warmth to the retarded children she met in the course of her charitable activities. And she was invariably kind to me whenever my duties as a mother conflicted with my responsibilities as her secretary. When my son, Kevin, had hepatitis, she not only sent him leftover roast beef and extra blankets—well-meaning gestures even if somewhat inappropriate—but she also was careful to send me home on the dot of five or even earlier every evening, saying, "Your son needs you, Barbara."

She also went out of her way to help my daughter, Kathleen . . . although I was not especially pleased at the result. Kathleen had been living with her father in Holland and had fallen in love with a Dutch boy. She was seventeen, and I wanted her to come back to this country; she wanted to live on her own in Holland so she could be near her boyfriend. I explained this whole situation to Mrs. Kennedy, who had always taken an interest in my children. She sent them postcards when she was in Europe, made sure they were invited out on the boat in Hyannis Port, and listened sympathetically when I had problems with them. When I told her about this one, she volunteered to talk to Kathleen, who was with me for the summer.

So one sunny morning, I sent Kathleen up to Mrs. Kennedy's bedroom, where she stayed for a long time. When she finally came back down, I heard Mrs. Kennedy calling down the stairs after her, "Remember you are not alone. You have someone of importance on your side." It seemed that when Kathleen began to talk about the situation herself, Mrs. Kennedy came down firmly on the side of young love and urged Kathleen to go back to her boyfriend! The story made her think of her own life, the boy she had fallen in love with when she was seventeen, the years she had loved Joe Kennedy but had to keep it a secret, seeing him only when their joint ingenuity could invent a way. She had a bit of a glow as she explained to me, "Like Kathleen, I was only seventeen, and Mr. Kennedy and I were not supposed to have dates. He was a manager of the tennis team at Boston Latin School, so he arranged for the team to play at Concord, where my uncle lived. So he went there with the tennis team, and I visited my uncle that weekend, and no one was the wiser." Even in her eighties, Mrs. Kennedy had a very romantic heart.

Perhaps the only valid conclusion about Mrs. Kennedy's behavior was that she was in many ways a typical elderly grandmother. She loved her grandchildren, often without understanding them . . . and sometimes even without liking them.

She enjoyed seeing them all together, and she liked to hear about their achievements and accomplishments. She always made a special effort to send gifts and cards when one of them graduated from high school or college. She congratulated Ted's children Kara and Teddy on their progress in learning French. She was pleased and amused when Bobby Shriver became an entrepreneur and had his own clambake business in Hyannis Port; she was also impressed when he went to work for a Baltimore newspaper, and wrote him jokingly to say her only objection to his job was that he would now know more about the news than she did. She wrote Ethel's daughter Kathleen, the first of her generation to marry, a lovely letter saying how much pleasure she took in knowing that Kathleen had a happy marriage.

I'll always remember a conversation we had one day when Mrs. Kennedy was not feeling well. Her eyes were bothering her so that she couldn't even read the papers, and she was also suffering from a bad stomach upset. When I went up to her room, she was lying on her faded chaise, facing away from the bright light reflected from the ocean, staring at the walls of her shabby Palm Beach bedroom. After a long silence, she said, "Why do people go on living and living when they get so old and don't feel well and can't enjoy anything?" More silence. Then she asked wearily, "Do you see anything for me to live for?"

I answered, "I don't know, Mrs. Kennedy; I think it would be nice to see how your grandchildren turn out."

After another long pause, she retorted, "Oh, I don't care about them."

The sad truth was that she had been so fully invested in her children that there was little left over for the next generation. All of her hopes and dreams had been wrapped up in her nine children, and now in her old age, many of those dreams were lost forever. Through the fates of her nine children—four now dead and one permanently institutionalized—she had suffered so much pain and loss, been through so many highs and lows, that she simply didn't have the emotional energy to start all over again with her twenty-nine grandchildren.

10

Rose Kennedy ... Alone

R ose Kennedy was a familiar figure to millions of people the world over. She was the matriarch of a large family; just a gathering of her grandchildren could fill up an ordinary living room. She was one of the wealthiest women in the United States, able to surround herself comfortably with servants and the usual entourage of the rich, had she chosen to do so. Yet the way I remember seeing her most often was all alone.

When I first went to work for Mrs. Kennedy, I was amazed by her solitude. In Palm Beach, even when the house was full of visitors, Mrs. Kennedy kept to her own schedule, and neither her children nor her grandchildren were allowed to disrupt it. In Hyannis Port, the compound was full of people all summer long, but few of them ever entered Mrs. Kennedy's carefully ordered world.

I believe Mrs. Kennedy's lonely life evolved out of a combination of her habits and preferences, and the fears of her family and friends about upsetting or distressing her. Over the years, people simply stopped making the effort to include her in their activities or to join her in hers. She, too, clearly lost the desire to join them. In many ways, her life was that of a recluse.

181

Of course, when I knew Mrs. Kennedy, she was old and in precarious health, which may have caused her to become more isolated. But I suspect that she had always preferred her independence. For example, she liked to reminisce about her trips with Joe Kennedy and how they always went their separate ways. In New York, he would stay at the Waldorf-Astoria Towers and she would stay at the Plaza; in Paris, he would stay somewhere convenient to a golf course and she would stay near the couture houses. She said they would meet for dinner or an evening at the theater and talk about what they had done that day. She attributed the fact that they always got along so well together to their frequent separations and independent existences. Her daughter Jean said her mother's independence was her own first introduction to the ideals of the women's movement. It might perhaps be the case that Mrs. Kennedy's attitudes were shaped by the necessity of adjusting to a husband who was often away from home for long periods and who was rumored to be involved with numerous other women. If so, she had long since made a virtue of necessity and had in reality come to prefer being alone most of the time.

It was easy to see that most of her pleasures came from things she did alone. Her daily swim, which had started out as a therapeutic measure, had turned into one of her greatest sources of comfort and well-being. But she preferred to swim alone, or with me, because with me she could completely drop her guard. Her newspaper reading was another solitary pleasure. She read several papers every day, went through them carefully, and clipped some articles to save. But she never discussed what she had read with anyone else and never consulted the files of articles she had clipped. She simply liked the feeling that she was still keeping up, even though she rarely shared the results.

In fact, Mrs. Kennedy at the time I knew her was one of the most inner-directed people I had ever met. Occasionally, in matters of etiquette, she might be concerned with what other people thought. But mostly she did things for her own reasons and paid little heed to the opinions of others. Even her efforts to stay abreast of the latest slang, or her questions to "Moucher" about the correct way to address her son, the Duke of Devonshire, were not induced by any worry about what other people would say if she didn't know. It was important to *her*, for her own image of herself, that she know these things.

Her desire to keep up with the world and to keep improving herself was totally remarkable for someone her age. When I first began to type quotations to go in her "expressions" book, a fat black three-ring notebook, I assumed that the book represented a species of busywork—something that made her feel like she was still a part of the world of the famous and powerful—and would never be used. I was dead wrong. She studied those pages of expressions frequently, sometimes pinning them to a towel or the front of her bathrobe so she would readily see them and work on memorizing them. Once I remember driving home at the end of the day and catching sight of her sitting under a tree with a large scarf covering most of her face, studiously poring over a sheet of expressions like a schoolgirl cramming for an exam.

She didn't just work on her expressions in English, mind you. She also studied them in French so she would be prepared for social events during her European trips or when she met foreigners in Washington. She worked hard at keeping up her French. Each week, while she had her hour-long massage, she put French-language records on the phonograph and listened to such things as excerpts from *Madame Bovary* or a historical account of the reign of Louis XV, to improve her French vocabulary and practice her comprehension skills. She liked to practice speaking French, too. Once she wrote a very funny letter to her grandson Teddy about her attempts to speak French to some distinguished visitor she met at a cocktail party Pat Lawford gave in New York. Intimidated by the man's perfect English, Mrs. Kennedy claimed she hardly dared to say "Bon soir" to him, but she did pluck up her courage to ask him what she needed to practice before her next trip to Paris. She concluded humorously that he kept going on in perfect English, and "I was very mad." It's easy to smile at the imagined scene —we all know how haughty the French can be about attempts to speak their language. But how many eighty-five-year-olds do you know who would have been so determined to try to improve themselves and their accent?

Mrs. Kennedy lived by a stoic philosophy. She never complained, and she genuinely did her best to accept whatever life brought her, including the trials of old age. Perhaps there was a bit of the New England Puritan about her, too. She thought it was unnecessary to spend money on the staff or the other conveniences that could make her life more comfortable . . . it seemed to me that she believed life was not meant to be a comfortable journey. In fact, she never did anything just because she enjoyed it. She really did like to travel, but she always needed an excuse to do it: She needed to buy clothes in Paris to uphold the standards set for her by her husband, or she had to see the eye doctor in Washington, or a European trip would give her the opportunity to polish her French. She had the same attitudes toward going to a play or concert or museum. In actual fact, she enjoyed it greatly, but she rationalized it to herself as a duty to keep up with cultural events. I remember that she encouraged me to go to New York and see a play, not because it would be fun, but because it would be a good experience for my daughter. According to her philosophy, it was all right to do anything for your children (including let them have fun), but that principle didn't apply to one's self. Mrs. Kennedy's satisfaction—perhaps even her happiness—came from the knowledge of having done her duty.

Of course, in this rather demanding view of life, she was supported by her deep religious beliefs. In many ways, the Catholic religion was the organizing principle of Mrs. Kennedy's life. It helped her organize her time; she created a schedule that revolved around her daily attendance at mass. It organized her beliefs and gave her a coherent outlook on life. Most deeply, it organized her expectations of the future.

Mrs. Kennedy was one of the few people I've ever known who seemed absolutely unafraid of death. Unlike many people her age, she rarely spoke about it—didn't talk about "when I am gone" or refuse to plan for the future on the grounds that

184

she might not live to see it. But when the subject of death came up, she seemed perfectly comfortable with it. I remember once in Palm Beach, Mrs. Kennedy and I went to the pool for our daily swim when it started to storm, with thunder and lightning. I was apprehensive about getting in the water, but Mrs. Kennedy got right in and called to me, "Come on in! Don't be a ninny!" I saw another bolt of lightning and must have looked like I was about to depart (I probably was) because she added gaily, "Don't you want to stick around and hear my last words?" Another time she wanted to swim in the ocean during a shark scare. "I'm not afraid of the sharks," she said firmly. "I've been swimming here for years." "Well," I answered, "I am! And with my luck, the shark would go for me and you'd swim in to shore." She laughed and said, "Where do you want me to send your check?"

Once Mrs. Kennedy thought there might be something wrong with her heart. She was taking her afternoon nap, and suddenly she called me to come to her. "My heart is making funny noises," she said without the slightest trace of anxiety or self-pity. "Please come listen to it." I put my ear over her chest but didn't notice anything unusual. Within ten or fifteen minutes, she called me again to say her heart was thumping wildly. This time I telephoned her doctor, and he told me to bring her right in to his office. I helped her get ready, and she insisted on getting dressed up as if she were going to a social event. She got all excited about the whole thing; it seemed that she relished the drama of having something really wrong with her, without having the slightest fear of the consequences. As it turned out, the doctor could find nothing wrong at all. I thought she seemed just a tiny bit disappointed that the drama was all over.

This blitheness about her health and safety was the result of her deep religious beliefs rather than a conviction of her invulnerability. In 1975 and '76, she spent quite a bit of time planning for the eventuality of her death. She was not morbid, and in fact she never even mentioned the word. But many of her activities revolved around getting things in order for the next generation. That was part of the reason for the obsessive visits to the attic and continual inventory of all her possessions.

She was giving many of the most valuable of her things to the next generation. Jean Smith was given a lovely vermeil tea set that Joe Kennedy had purchased in London at a Red Cross auction during World War II. He later discovered it had been donated by the King and Queen, and in appreciation of his generous bid, they added a vermeil tray to go with the tea set. Ethel was given an expensive painting of pink flowers that had always hung in Mrs. Kennedy's bedroom. Ted got the silver, and Jean was given an antique table. Mrs. Kennedy sold some of the jewelry she no longer had occasion to wear, and she decided to put other valuables in the bank vault, out of harm's way. That was what she did with President Kennedy's hand-written draft of his inaugural address that used to hang in the den at the Palm Beach House.

She also spent countless hours tinkering with the provisions of her will. The outlines were generally clear and stable; she left some of her estate to benefit the retarded, and the rest was divided up, more or less equally, among the family. It was the minor provisions that gave her the most trouble. For example, she debated for days about whether she should leave her old and not very well-to-do friend Mrs. Marie Greene $5,000 in her will or not, in light of the fact that Joe Kennedy, always the thoughtful provider, had arranged an annual payment of $5,000 for her lifetime. Did that mean Marie had already been given enough, or did it mean Mrs. Kennedy ought to be sure to make her this one last gift? And what about the nephew who was a priest? Should he get less than the other nieces and nephews, since he had no children to provide for? And since she was leaving Caroline and John their father's desk, shouldn't she de- duct a sum equivalent to its value from the amount she was leaving Jackie? Was her estate big enough to afford a $25,000 legacy to her one living brother? These questions went round and round in her head, and she was constantly sending notes and making calls to the New York office about such matters. She asked them to handle drawing up the changes and sometimes also to explain them to those most concerned. As she put it, it was "quite an emotional experience" for her to do it. Her will was continually redrafted. I remember when a new will was brought to the house in the summer of 1976, and Mrs. Kennedy asked Jeannette to witness it; Jeannette said it was the fifth time she had been a witness.

This activity bespoke a concern about the future of her family, not a fear of her own death, which she faced serenely. Her faith in an afterlife was rock-solid, as indeed was her faith in all the beliefs of her church. She observed all its rituals and respected its demands. She regularly had mass said for all of her dear departed, and her own prayers were frequent and heartfelt. To me, her relationship with the Church was epitomized by her letters to members of the Catholic clergy; her invariable closing was "Your respectful child."

Interestingly, the fact that Mrs. Kennedy was alone so much of the time didn't mean that she had forgotten how to have fun. She had a lively sense of humor, which always made our conversations enjoyable. She giggled a lot, and she was a gratifying audience for funny stories. I remember telling her about my trip back from picking Joan up at the airport, when the alarm on the Lincoln started up and couldn't be turned off. My description of how we went through sedate Palm Beach with the alarm wailing and attracting the attention of every passerby really tickled her, and she laughed a long time at the conclusion of the story, in which Joan and I were driven back to North Ocean Boulevard in a pickup truck by one of the men who worked at the garage where we took the car to be fixed. She had a keen sense of the ridiculous, which must have been a help on more than one occasion in the life she led.

She could also "play," in the sense psychologists mean when they describe emotionally healthy human beings. Music was a particularly good outlet for this, as her duets in the kitchen with Nellie or her own renditions of "Sweet Adeline" on the piano attested. I especially remember one time, that last summer I worked for her, when she confounded everyone by her high spirits. Teddy was around that weekend, and Doris Kearns, the esteemed biographer, and her husband, Richard Goodwin (once a Kennedy staffer), were in town. Somehow, the whole group, including Nellie, the cook, ended up going on Saturday night to the Irish Pub, a quaint spot in Hyannis with old wooden tables and live Irish music. Mrs. Kennedy threw herself into the spirit of the evening and began singing along with all the old Irish ballads she loved so well. She enjoyed herself so much that she didn't get home until the early hours of Sunday morning. Her doctor couldn't get over it. Only a few days before that, she had been quite sick, and he was thinking of sending her back to New England Baptist Hospital for observation and tests. Then the next thing he knew, she was out carousing until two o'clock in the morning! Surprisingly the outing didn't seem to do her a bit of harm . . . probably because she was having so much fun all the time. She once told me, "Never pass up an opportunity to have some fun. You never know what's around the corner."

Despite her inner reserves, there were times when it was obvious to me that Mrs. Kennedy was not just alone but also lonely. I remember particularly one Christmas in Palm Beach when none of the family was there with her. She had hoped that some of the children and grandchildren might decide to come, so she bought a tree as usual several days before the holiday and set the staff to work decorating it. "I've never done it myself," she explained to me. "The men always did it." I never knew who she meant by "the men," an expression I had often heard her use. For example, once when I went to pick her up at the airport, she said as we were leaving, "Shall we get the luggage ourselves or shall we send the men for it?" I often wished that there *were* some helpful men around to do the heavy jobs, but in fact, Dennis was rarely on the premises, and not particularly helpful when he was, and Jim Connors, the guard, worked only a few nights a week. So most of the work fell on me and the elderly women, like Mam'selle and Nellie, who worked for Mrs. Kennedy.

Once we had the tree up and the house decorated, it did look lovely. The lights lining the long entryway had colored bulbs, and the small trees around the front patio were also covered with bright twinkling lights. Large red poinsettias lined the front entrance hall, and in the living room there was not only a tree but a number of plants that had been sent as gifts, including a beautiful huge white poinsettia from Jackie. At night especially, the house had quite a festive look.

But no one ever came to spend that Christmas with Mrs. Kennedy. On Christmas Eve, she ordered Dennis to take down the tree and take it to the local Catholic school where it could be enjoyed by all the children. Since she had the habit of opening any present she received the moment it came, there were no packages left behind . . . nothing for Mrs. Kennedy to look forward to opening on Christmas morning. I had a small surprise for her. I had asked a friend who made hats from palm leaves to whip one up for Mrs. Kennedy to wear in swimming on sunny days. I put it, before I left that night, by her plate in the big dining room, set for just one person to have breakfast on Christmas morning. I felt sad as I walked out the door and home to my own family, where our Christmas Eve celebration was waiting. I called her the next day to wish her a Merry Christmas and was relieved to hear that she was going out to the Wrightsmans for Christmas dinner.

I couldn't really blame Mrs. Kennedy's children and grandchildren for this state of affairs. I knew she had turned down their invitations to visit with monotonous regularity. She returned their Christmas gifts, and she often scolded their extravagance whenever they attempted to do something for her. If someone brought her flowers or sent her a plant, she would tell them they ought to save their money, since they never knew when it might be needed. When family members telephoned, they were admonished to call at a different time so it wouldn't cost so much money.

Still, I thought it was a shame that she had nobody around her who really understood her and her habits. Even her domestic staff was of fairly recent origin. Nellie had previously worked for Ted, and Mam'selle had worked for Pat, but neither of them had worked for Mrs. Kennedy for very long when I arrived on the scene. Jeannette, too, had only been there a few years longer than I had. In fact, of all the people I met when I first worked in the Kennedy house in 1969, not a single one was there when

I returned in 1974. Mrs. Kennedy had none of those long-term associations that can make daily life at once more comfortable and more comforting.

It bothered me to realize that I was one of the most stable elements of Mrs. Kennedy's existence. Dave Powers, whose sense of humor had made him one of Jack Kennedy's most valued aides, once kiddingly told me I ought to be in the *Guinness Book of World Records* for staying in the job longer than anyone else ever did. Previously the turnover in the position had been notorious. I remember telling my predecessor, Jay Sanderson, over a friendly lunch several years after I started to work for Mrs. Kennedy that she was thinking about writing another book. "What's she going to call it," asked Jay pointedly, "*Secretaries I Have Known?*"

Certainly Mrs. Kennedy could be difficult to work for, sometimes demanding and imperious, often stubborn and irrational. But I always knew I received at least as much as I gave. I was warmed by her charm, enjoyed her company, and took satisfaction in knowing I was really able to help her. And I felt she was always a positive influence. I remember the times that she commented on my bad posture as I stood in her bedroom or sat at my desk; although her remarks could make me feel like a child, they also made me aware of my posture and helped me improve it. She encouraged me to watch my weight and to be careful about what I ate. She subjected me to the same scrutiny she used on herself, commenting favorably on my long curly eyelashes but explaining that I was using a foundation that was too light for the color of my skin. She gave me a little bottle of her own darker shade, so I could see for myself the improvement it made. She noticed what I wore to work and gave me compliments on outfits she thought were particularly becoming. She tried to break me of the habit of saying "okay," which she thought was too informal. She was a perfectionist herself, and she applied those same high standards to those around her. It's one of the reasons I knew she cared about me, too.

More effective than any of her specific comments was the

example she set for me. Here was an eighty-five-year-old woman listening to recordings of Proust's works in order to improve her French vocabulary and accent; carefully eating a ripe banana every day for the potassium to improve her health; buying the latest makeup so she could stay in style; going out to campaign in front of thousands of people even when she was half-sick, just because she thought her son needed her. She was so interested, so vital, so determined to keep improving herself. Those traits are rare at any age, but particularly unusual for a woman in her eighties. When you thought about the sorrow she had borne, and saw how free she was from self-pity or constant recrimination against fate, how determined to be cheerful and happy in her daily life—well, Mrs. Kennedy was a constant inspiration to me.

Unfortunately it was gradually becoming clear, both to me and to Mrs. Kennedy, that she didn't need a secretary. As her health deteriorated, she could take on fewer and fewer engagements of any sort. And she didn't really handle her own affairs any longer. The New York office already took care of most of her bills and her business. When I first went to work for her, Mrs. Kennedy made several spirited efforts to get things back in her own hands, writing to Tom Walsh in New York about how she could take a load off his staff by paying her own bills. But within a few years, she had lost the energy and the interest to try to find out about her own financial position, and she was quite content to let New York take care of it all. I realized it would be just as easy for them to take care of her mail, too, since very little of it was personal. Mrs. Kennedy had got to the point where she couldn't even manage the two or three letters a day I would show her. A simple note from a friend would throw her into high anxiety, bringing on headaches and stomach upsets. And most of the time, her eyes were so bad that she couldn't read her own correspondence, her hands so shaky she couldn't write her own replies, or even her familiar notes in my shorthand book to tell me what ought to be done the next morning.

What Mrs. Kennedy needed was not a secretary, but a combination nurse and companion. That would meet her needs better, and I knew it. Eventually, she knew it, too. That was a hard thing for her to acknowledge, partly (I like to think) because she and I had developed a supportive and even devoted relationship, and she hated to see me go. Partly, it was also that giving up a secretary was symbolic of the end of her genuine independence. Henceforth, the New York office and the family would make all the important decisions about her life.

Another woman might have kept quiet about the situation, letting it drift on as long as possible. But that was not Mrs. Kennedy's way. As soon as she faced the fact herself that I had very few secretarial duties left, she was determined to act on her realization. She was never a person to sweep things under the carpet.

One day that last summer I was with her in Hyannis Port, she walked into my office at a particularly frantic moment. It was not long before the big annual Labor Day bash, and Ethel's secretary had just called to say their outdoor man had quit: Did I know of someone who could get their lawn in shape? While I was trying to make calls about that, I was also coping with the arrangements for the arrival of the Smith family and their maid, and taking a call from the governess hired by the Senator. She was with the Senator and the two older children on the boat at a Nantucket dock, and she wanted me to check on Joan and Patrick, who had been left behind in the house. I promised I would find the time to jump in the car and drive out to the house to see how they were getting along.

Mrs. Kennedy watched and listened without comment for a few minutes as I struggled to deal with the complications of the Kennedy family. Finally she said in her clear, carrying voice, "One consolation in all this . . . I'm leaving this very soon!" I couldn't think of a tactful reply to her almost cheerful view of her own death, and the moments ticked by. Finally she concluded, "If you're smart, you'll leave, too."

With that clue to what was going on in her mind, I was not surprised when she began to ask me a few days later about how much mail there was to handle, whether I was sending it to the New York office, and other questions about my work. I felt I owed it to her to answer honestly, to let her confirm the fact that most of my time was spent coping with the family and in acting as a companion to her. "You'd probably be better off with a second maid or a nurse, Mrs. Kennedy," I explained. After a pause, she agreed. From then on, we shared the tacit assumption that I was leaving sometime in the near future, and it was just a matter of weeks before I made my plans and told Mrs. Kennedy I would quit when she left Hyannis Port that fall.

The remaining weeks were hard for us both. Sometimes I felt so sad for her that I was on the verge of volunteering to stay on and look after her as a nurse, even though it was not the right kind of work for me and certainly the wrong career path for me to take. Then some incident between us would remind me that Rose Kennedy was not a woman who would accept other people's pity; she didn't want it and, in the end, didn't need it. Ultimately we both accepted that my departure was inevitable.

I finally gave notice, and it was arranged that I would stay on a few weeks after Mrs. Kennedy left Hyannis Port in the fall to catch up with the correspondence and close the house, and that would be the end of my tenure as secretary. In those last days we had together, Mrs. Kennedy was invariably kind and thoughtful. She told me that I was always welcome to stay in either house or the New York apartment whenever I wanted to, and she frequently asked about my plans for my son's education for that last year of high school. Once she simply said, "You're always in my prayers, dear."

Then it was time for Mrs. Kennedy to leave and for us to say good-bye. True to style, she refused to enter into any emotional scene. I lined up on the front veranda with the others: Arthur, Jeannette, and Nellie, who had come north that summer to help with the cooking. Everything was just the same as it was every fall . . . with one exception. This time, Mrs. Kennedy didn't kiss me good-bye. I knew it was just her way of maintaining her self-control.

We all chatted with Mrs. Kennedy for a few minutes, and

Nellie said to her, in her bluff Scots burr, "You've had the best of everything, haven't you, Mrs. Kennedy?"

"Yes, yes," she answered, "I've had the best of everything, and I've also had the worst of everything."

Nellie and I looked at one another then, as if to say, "And so she has."

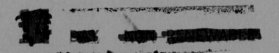